The Game of
Singles in Tennis

By the same authors:

The Game of Doubles in Tennis
Stroke Production in the Game of Tennis

The Game of Singles in Tennis

by William F. Talbert and Bruce S. Old

Drawings by Katharine D. Old and Ed Vebell
Diagrams by Stephen P. Baldwin

Revised Edition

J. B. LIPPINCOTT COMPANY
Philadelphia and New York

The drawings by Ed Vebell on pages 40 and 142 and some of the text and
captions on these pages have appeared in somewhat different form in *Sports
Illustrated* magazine and in *Sports Illustrated Book of Tennis,* J. B. Lippincott Company, Philadelphia and New York, copyright © 1958, 1959, 1960
by Time Inc.

The diagrams on pages 45, 47, 69, 88–89, 106–7, and 126–27 and some of the
accompanying text have appeared in somewhat different form in *Sports
Illustrated* magazine, copyright © 1962 by Time Inc.

U.S. Library of Congress Cataloging in Publication Data

Talbert, William F
    The game of singles in tennis.

    1. Tennis—Singles. I. Old, Bruce S., joint author.
II. Title.
GV1002.7.T3   1976   796.34′227   76–40118
ISBN–0–397–01181–4

Contents

Forewords

Tennis is a game of intelligence, confidence, and skill. And one of the best ways to develop these qualities in yourself is to follow the recommendations that Bill Talbert and Bruce Old give you in *The Game of Singles in Tennis*. It is above all a practical, straightforward book, and it will give you invaluable instruction in strategy and stroke production that will stick with you throughout your tennis-playing life. I think it's an excellent basic book on singles. I commend it to you.

September, 1976

Chris Evert

I consider *The Game of Singles in Tennis* to be must reading for every tennis player, expert or beginner. Every player can learn from it because Bill Talbert and Bruce Old have put into words what many top players know instinctively but may have taken years to learn: that certain offensive and defensive tactics will give you a winning edge over your opponent on almost every shot. They also tell you *why* these tactics work and how to make them a part of your own game, and the authors' insights are based on clear, logical, real-game situations. So if you really want to improve your game—and get more enjoyment out of this fast and beautiful game of tennis —read *The Game of Singles*. It can make you into the kind of tennis player you want to be.

September, 1976

Vitas Gerulaitis

The Game of
Singles in Tennis

Introduction

The purpose of this book is to attempt to present in a detailed yet readable manner the basic fundamentals of the game of singles in tennis. While there have been a number of books written dealing with stroke production and with certain phases of singles play, no truly comprehensive presentation of the many facets of this great game has ever been published.

The authors believe that most players, whether they are of the tournament circuit variety, or occasional weekend enthusiasts, or merely beginners, can profit to a marked degree by a study of the game. In this way players can develop their games so that they will habitually try the proper shots at the correct moment and thus utilize their own particular talents to maximum advantage. Naturally, talents and styles of play vary, so that we have attempted to cover the subject in a manner which will be helpful to all types of players.

To assist the reader, a number of drawings and diagrams have been included to illustrate clearly the methods of stroke production, and the positions of the players and the movement of the ball in complete singles points taken from actual matches. A typical example of the latter is given in figure 1 in order to present the method and the symbols utilized.

While it may seem like wishing for the stars, it is our hope that this book will assist in some small way the development of singles play in the United States, to the end that we will regain our former enviable position as the producer of the best players in this great international game.

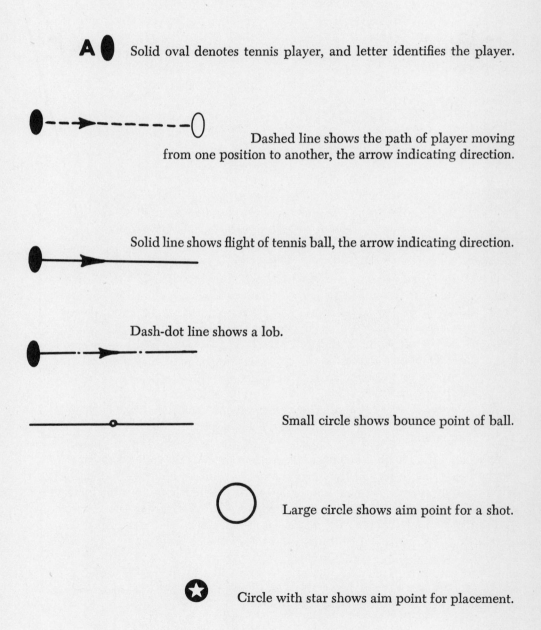

A Solid oval denotes tennis player, and letter identifies the player.

Dashed line shows the path of player moving from one position to another, the arrow indicating direction.

Solid line shows flight of tennis ball, the arrow indicating direction.

Dash-dot line shows a lob.

Small circle shows bounce point of ball.

Large circle shows aim point for a shot.

Circle with star shows aim point for placement.

Figure 1

Diagram Method

This figure illustrates the method used to diagram points in this book. It also serves to show how two mistakes by player A cost this particular point.

Player A serves deep to the backhand of player B and then rushes the net to volley the return. Receiver B hits a cross-court backhand return of service which server A volleys back, but, in doing so, A makes the first mistake by not hitting it sufficiently deep. This gives receiver B, who had retreated to the defensive base line position, an opportunity to move forward and take the offense. Server A then makes a second and final mistake by moving very rapidly to the right to cover a possible cross-court return. While this move is in the proper direction, player A makes the common fatal mistake of overcommitting by running too far cross court. By continuing to move, A is not in a balanced position from which to cover the backhand as well as the forehand side. In moving forward, player B notes this situation carefully and decides to place a passing shot down the line behind the moving net player. As shown, this brings well-deserved success.

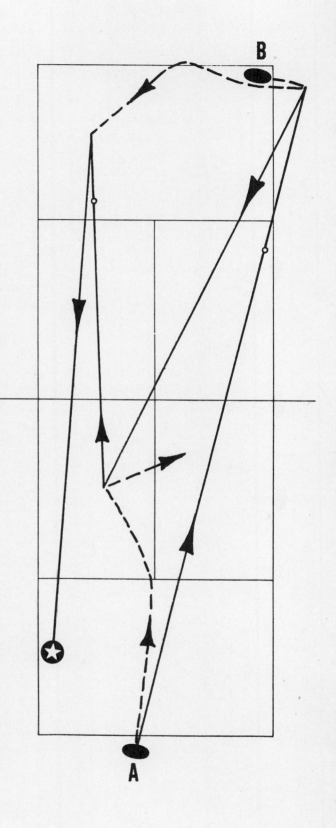

The Greatest
of Individual Sports

There is really little or no doubt about it—the game of singles in tennis represents the ultimate in individual international sports.

Since we wish to avoid at all cost alienating at the outset any readers who are golf, swimming, boxing, track, bowling, billiards, squash, fencing, or wrestling enthusiasts, let us immediately consider the justification for this claim. Those who need convincing should ponder the following:

It is international.

Tennis is the most international of all sports. Singles is played the world over by both sexes, young and old. It is played in big cities and small towns, at exclusive clubs and public playgrounds, indoors and outdoors, by people from all walks of life. The smooth, rhythmic, intensely athletic nature of the game provides absorbing interest not only to the contestants but also to the gallery, making it a top spectator sport everywhere. Some forty nations compete each year for the renowned Davis Cup, symbol of the world's championship among the nations. It is not unusual to have representatives from twenty nations competing for the famous Wimbledon and United States singles titles.

It requires skill and speed.

Tennis is a game which goes true to form. To play through a best-of-five-sets singles match leaves little chance for doubt as to the more skillful player—luck has essentially no bearing when the ball will have to be hit over the net some one thousand times in a match! Stroke production, style, speed, footwork, timing, tactics, and accuracy cannot but assert themselves over this extended period of chasing and stroking a ball which sometimes travels at speeds around 100 miles per hour. And, to further accentuate the need for skill, the ball often takes erratic bounces, forcing changes of plans to be calculated with phenomenal rapidity. Tennis is truly a game of tenths of seconds and tenths of inches played at breakneck speed.

It requires generalship.

The great Anthony Wilding once said, "Perfect style, inexhaustible stamina, even the best strokes are of no avail if the brain that governs the hand is not taking stock of strategical positions and planning moves by which winning coups may be achieved." Ingenious strategy and tactics give infinite variety to the game and bring about the possibility of upsets. When opponents possess nearly equal stroke capability, the match is won by the player utilizing the superior generalship, the player who studies the style, strokes, and psychology of an opponent in order to learn strengths and weaknesses and anticipate moves. With this knowledge a player can feed the shots, spin, change of pace, depth and angles, and utilize the position play needed to upset the opponent's game and thus win the match. He or she can also sense just that moment when the tide of the battle is turning, when a change in tactics is required, and how to seize and exploit every opportunity. To accomplish this requires tremendous and undivided powers of concentration. Tennis is certainly the most intellectual of active sports.

It requires stamina.

William T. Tilden once said, "Tennis puts an athlete under the hardest physical, mental, and nervous strain of any game played by mankind." Unequivocal backing for this statement has come from numerous two- and three-sport athletes. It was concurred in, for example, by Joe Hunt, who played varsity football, and by Tony Trabert, who played varsity basketball, when each was at the top of U.S. tennis. Tennis requires stamina not only because of the great amount of running, quick starts, stops, and changes of direction over a two- to three-hour period, but also because the generalship one must exercise places on the system a mental and a nervous strain which serves to compound severely the fatigue problems. Think of the total number of decisions involving complex factors of stroke production and tactics which a tennis player must make within a half-second time allowance during the course of a five-set match! No wonder tennis players are completely exhausted after a tough encounter and find it difficult to be at top form all the way through a tournament.

It requires courage.

One of the qualities which stands out in great tennis players, whether club or world champions, is an unquenchable spirit of courage. It is exemplified by the will to win and the determination to overcome all odds. Could anyone ever watch a match played by a William M. Johnston, a Bitsy Grant, or a Ted Schroeder without having indelibly imprinted on his mind a vision of sheer courage? Just when all seems lost and a tennis player is too tired to think, or to toss the ball up for the next serve, he or she must be able to reach down for that last ounce of reserve strength and fight all the way back. There is no other way to explain such comebacks as the famous Davis Cup victory of Don Budge over Baron Gottfried Von Cramm after being down 1–4 in the fifth set. The great Norman E. Brookes and Henri Cochet were at their best just when they seemed hopelessly beaten. They were as cool under fire as the proverbial iceberg. And do you know the story of the 1921 Davis Cup match when Tilden played despite a dangerously infected foot? He promptly lost the first two sets and was within two points of defeat before winning the third set 7–5 from the Japanese star, Zenzo Shimizu. Although every step was painful, and the physician who lanced the infection during the rest period advised his default, Tilden refused to quit. He held on grimly and finally won in five sets. History is replete with such incidents of courage on the tennis court.

It has a tradition of sportsmanship.

Singles breeds sportsmanship. When playing without an umpire, players must call all balls on their side of the net. It is an unwritten rule that one always gives the opponent the benefit of the doubt on close decisions. During a club match it is rare that you fail to find a receiver calling a shot good, only to have the striker refuse to accept the call in the belief that the ball was out. Perhaps the most celebrated incident of this type occurred in a Davis Cup match. J. C. Parke of England hit an overhead smash away for game, set, and Davis Cup match against Norman E. Brookes of Australia. However, Parke walked over to the umpire and informed him that his racket touched the net on his follow-through. After some discussion the umpire awarded the point to Brookes, who proceeded to take advantage of this life-giving break to lift his game and win the match, ultimately giving Australia the Davis Cup.

The tradition of the game also calls for courtesy, a minimum of temperament display, and no alibis. The previously mentioned incident concerning Tilden's infected foot was never revealed by Tilden himself. It came to light only after his death through the writings of Vincent Richards, who was present in the dressing room during the rest period visit of the physician.

It is available to all.

The existence of tennis courts all over the world, coupled with the inexpensive nature of tennis equipment, permits all people to play singles. The fact that one can transport one's equipment easily, and is able to get plenty of exercise in one hour, adds much to the appeal of the game. And you do not have to collect a team—you need only two people to play.

Now combine these multiple attributes of broad international competition, skill, speed, generalship, stamina, courage, sportsmanship, and easy availability to all, and you have in the game of singles in tennis the greatest of individual sports. How can one think otherwise in contemplating the pleasures and intricacies of the game?

Every reader must understand that singles is a game in which he or she might excel, because its infinite variety makes for champions of remarkable diversities of style and physique. Be you beginner, weekend player, or champion you can inspire yourself to greater heights by sitting back in your easy chair, closing your eyes, and visualizing the following historical parade: the smooth, sporting perfection of the Dohertys, the tactical guile of the ageless Brookes, the gallant appeal of Wilding, the steadiness of William Larned, the flashing serve of Maurice McLoughlin, the fighting determination of Little Bill Johnston, the all-around genius of Tilden, the daring of cat-like Cochet, the deft volley of Richards, the machinelike precision of René Lacoste, the brilliant dash of Jean Borotra, the rocketing drives of Ellsworth Vines, the awe-inspiring backhand of Budge, the unbelievable scrambling and retrieving ability of Bitsy Grant, the great "big game" of Jack Kramer, the stupendous, overpowering blasts of Pancho Gonzales, the impeccable ground strokes of ageless Ken Rosewall, the devastating all-court left-handed spin game of Grand Slammer Rod Laver, the sound and smooth winning power strokes of John Newcombe, and, finally, the totally aggressive forcing play employed continually and so effectively by Arthur Ashe and Jimmy Connors. Yes, this breath-taking picture of variety is bound to force you into an incredulous smile. Now top off your visions by adding as a background the shimmering tenseness and butterflies-in-the-stomach feeling associated with any final match, all the way from the local tennis club to the center court at Wimbledon. Thus inspired, you cannot help but resolve to work on, think about, and improve every aspect of your style in this wonderful game.

And, finally, you enterprising players should remember, the perfect singles player has not yet walked out on any tennis court!

2

The Great Players

Devotees of lawn tennis can thank a major in the British army for making the game into a worldwide sport. Tennis is traceable in one form or another all the way back to the ancient Greeks. The Romans played a form of it under the name of "Pila." And the nobles of France developed their own complex version, which is now known as court tennis. But the expense of the court for this game made it available to only a limited few. Thus, tennis all but died out in the nineteenth century.

Then along came Major Walton Clopton Wingfield with an idea for a game which he first described to some of his friends in a booklet, "The Major's Game of Lawn Tennis"—dedicated to the party assembled at Nantclwyd in December 1873. The basic inventive thought was to provide a simple, inexpensive court which would make the game available to the public. Major Wingfield applied for a patent on a portable court for playing tennis February 23, 1874. He was awarded Letters Patent No. 685 on July 24, 1874.

The game spread with astounding speed around the world, largely because the British army adopted it enthusiastically as a barracks exercise. Thus, it appeared in the United States in 1874, India in 1875, Germany in 1876, France in 1877, and Australia in 1878. There have been remarkably few rule changes since these early days, a testimony to the soundness of the game.

The first great singles tournament was organized at Wimbledon in England in 1877. The first champion was Spencer W. Gore. Except for interruptions attributable to war, Wimbledon has been held ever since. This tradition is such a drawing card for players the world over that the tournament is usually considered the world's greatest.

The second most important singles tournament was inaugurated in the United States in 1881. That was the first year the United States National Championship was held by the United States Lawn Tennis Association. The first tournament was held in Newport, Rhode Island, and was won by Richard D. Sears. This great tournament has been staged every year since (except 1917) at various locations such as Newport, Philadelphia, and the West Side Tennis Club at Forest Hills, Long Island.

The world's third most famous singles encounter is the outgrowth of an inspired thought by one of the early tennis greats of the United States, Dwight F. Davis. While still a student at Harvard, Davis decided to present a trophy for a series of international team matches between the United States and the British Isles. He selected for his trophy of goodwill a large and beautiful silver bowl, which promptly became known as the Davis Cup. The importance of the concept was almost immediately expanded beyond the fondest dreams of the youthful Davis. The Davis Cup became a symbol not just of United States vs. Britain, but of international team supremacy as the tennis associations of the world readily adopted the idea. In addition it became a shining symbol of sportsmanship and of love of the game of tennis. No sports event in history has had such a favorable effect in fostering international goodwill and understanding as the Davis Cup. Play for the cup consists of a series of elimination rounds involving four singles and one doubles match in each round, with the winner requiring victories in three of the five matches. The nation winning the elimination series then plays the previous year's winner in the Challenge Round for the Davis Cup. Because this great series of matches has brought about competition between the world's best players throughout the years since the initial presentation in 1900, it has played a vital role in the development of the game by singles. By a bit of richly deserved justice, Davis was himself a member of the first winning team, contributing vital victories for the United States in both singles and doubles! In later life Davis also gained fame as a member of the Cabinet of President Calvin Coolidge.

The records of the nations over the years in Davis Cup competition are shown in Table I. The outstanding singles play of the United States and Australia is clearly evident. It is also evident that in Davis Cup play, even the small nations can excel.

In order to select the top singles players of history, it is necessary to study their records with particular emphasis on the basis of their performances in the three aforementioned events, the Wimbledon, United States, and Davis Cup Challenge Round contests. When this is done, it becomes obvious that it is possible to omit from the list certain of the more recent greats because they turned professional after comparatively few key victories. Therefore, it was decided out of fairness, as well as for accuracy, that a fourth criterion for judgment be added. The best measure obtainable for performance by the professionals was that of top annual ranking, as no one or two tournaments appeared to be accepted as representing the championship. With this added factor, a listing of the best singles players of all time has been made, as shown in Table II.

From 1877 to date the game of singles has gone through continued development and improvement at the hands of these great players. Valuable assistance has, of course, been rendered by numerous coaches,

TABLE I

Davis Cup Challenge and Final Rounds

Nation	Number of Rounds	Number of Rounds Won	Number of Singles Matches Won	Percentage of Singles Matches Won
United States	48	24	99	54
Australia	38	23	82	52
Great Britain	16	9	40	64
France	9	6	19	53
Romania	3	0	3	25
Italy	2	0	1	12
Spain	2	0	2	25
India	2	0	0	0
Belgium	1	0	0	0
Japan	1	0	0	0
Mexico	1	0	0	0
W. Germany	1	0	0	0
S. Africa	1	1	4	100
Sweden	1	1	2	50
Czechoslovakia	1	0	2	50

students of the game, and writers. Deserving of special mention in this category are such people as Mercer Beasely, Wilfred Baddeley, Teach Tennant, J. Parmly Paret, Harry Hopman, Tom Stow, Dick Skeen, Allison Danzig, Fred Hawthorne, and others.

Let us trace the development of the game of singles by running through some of the interesting aspects of history. In this way a clear picture can be gained of the effect of each newly formulated attack and defense on the evolution of singles. While you will find that the game has gone through several phases, there is one solid foundation on which each new forward development is based. That foundation is speed, more and more speed—hitting the ball harder and sooner in order to make the attack more potent and the defense more difficult.

By the time the first Wimbledon tournament began in 1877, the original Marylebone Cricket Club tennis rules formulated in 1875 had been al-

TABLE II

Outstanding Men Singles Players

TOURNAMENT AND YEAR OF VICTORY

Name and Nationality	Wimbledon	United States	Davis Cup	Ranking Professional
William Renshaw (G.B.)	81, 82, 83, 84, 85, 86, 89			
Richard D. Sears (U.S.)		81, 82, 83, 84, 85, 86, 87		
Reginald F. Doherty (G.B.)	98, 99, 00		02, 03	
H. L. Doherty (G.B.)	02, 03, 04, 05, 06	03	03(2), 04(2), 05(2), 06(2)	
R. D. Wrenn (U.S.)		93, 94, 96, 97		
Malcolm Whitman (U.S.)		98, 99, 00	00(2), 02(2)	
William A. Larned (U.S.)		01, 02, 07, 08, 09, 10, 11	02, 03	
Norman E. Brookes (A.)	07, 14		07(2), 08, 09(2), 11(2), 12, 14	
Anthony F. Wilding (A.)	10, 11, 12, 13		07, 08, 09(2)	
William M. Johnston (U.S.)	23	15, 19	20(2), 21(2), 22(2), 23, 25(2), 26(2),	
Maurice E. McLoughlin (U.S.)		12, 13	13, 14(2)	
William T. Tilden (U.S.)	20, 21, 30	20, 21, 22, 23, 24, 25, 29	20(2), 21(2), 22(2), 23(2), 24(2), 25(2), 26, 27, 28, 29, 30	31, 32, 33
Jean Borotra (F.)	24, 26		29, 30, 32(2)	
J. René Lacoste (F.)	25, 28	26, 27	26, 27(2), 28	
Henri Cochet (F.)	27, 29	28	27, 28(2), 29(2), 30(2), 31(2), 32, 33	
H. Ellsworth Vines, Jr. (U.S.)	32	31, 32	32	34, 35, 36, 37, 38
Fred J. Perry (G.B.)	34, 35, 36	33, 34, 36	33(2), 34(2), 35(2), 36(2)	
J. Donald Budge (U.S.)	37, 38	37, 38	37(2), 38(2)	39, 40, 41, 42, 43, 44, 45
Robert L. Riggs (U.S.)	39	39, 41	38, 39	46, 47
John A. Kramer (U.S.)	47	46, 47	46(2), 47(2)	48, 49, 50, 51, 52
Frederick R. Schroeder, Jr. (U.S.)	49	42	46, 47(2), 48(2), 49(2), 51	
Richard A. Gonzales (U.S.)		48, 49	49(2)	53, 54, 55, 56, 57, 58, 59, 60, 61
Frank Sedgman (A.)	52	51, 52	50(2), 51(2), 52(2)	
Kenneth Rosewall (A.)		56, 70	53(1), 55(2), 56(2)	63, 64
Roy Emerson (A.)	64, 65	61, 64	61(2), 64(2), 65(1), 66(2), 67(2)	
Rodney Laver (A.)	61, 62, 68, 69	62, 69	60(2), 61(2), 62(2), 73(2)	65, 66, 67, 68
John Newcombe (A.)	67, 70, 71	67, 73	67(1), 73(2)	
Arthur Ashe (U.S.)	75	68	68(1), 69(2)	
Jimmy Connors (U.S.)	74	74		

tered. While these changes made the size and shape of the court and the location of service line as we know them today, they left the net high. It was only lowered from the original 4 feet at the center and 5 feet at the sides, to 3 feet 3 inches at the center. The astute Mr. Gore, first Wimbledon champion, used this to advantage by camping at the center of the net and volleying his way to the title. It turned out to be absurdly easy—the lob had not yet been invented! But the smarter members of the opposition did just that within the year, and Gore was quickly mastered in what was to prove the first of a long series of seesaw battles between net play and base line play. With the high net, the net player just could not get close enough to the net to volley down effectively without being overexposed to an easy lob. The most interesting point for the aspiring singles player to note about all this is that even the very first tennis tournaments were won by the players who used their heads.

The next three years represented the pat-ball era supreme. The difficulty of volleying in the face of the high net led to opponents' remaining on the base line. From this position they traded soft, graceful, unhurried shots. Proper manners and dress were the rule of the day.

Then came drama. The Renshaw brothers, William and Ernest, brought volleying back into the picture with a vengeance. To counteract the high net they volleyed from the service line, and to overcome the lob they developed the overhead smash. Against the leisurely base line play of the day this style was murderous. However, at about this moment there arrived on the scene H. F. Lawford, who developed a blistering top-spin drive from the base line. The two styles, volley and overhead vs. improved passing shots, in the persons of W. Renshaw vs. Lawford, fought it out for numerous titles over a period of some eight years. The attributes of their games were debated at length in the press and throughout tennis circles. In 1883, about the middle of the rivalry, the net was officially lowered to its present level of 3 feet in the center and 3 feet 6 inches at the sides. This served to intensify the debate, as it seemed bound to affect the outcome of the rivalry. While William Renshaw had won and continued to win most of the encounters, this did not convince everyone that the net was the place to play. In fact, over the next few years his brother, Ernest, and Wilfred Baddeley vied for the title from the base line, utilizing steady ground strokes.

This sort of tennis threw the game into a brief period of depression as far as spectator appeal was concerned. However, a new fresh wind of gale force was gathering on the horizon in the form of the greatest brother act in tennis history: R. F. and H. L. Doherty. For a decade their outstanding British and Davis Cup play so popularized the game as to assure tennis a role as a leading world sport for many years to come. Reggie (Big Do), two years the senior, and Laurie (Little Do) both went to Cambridge, where they were tennis heroes. One year after graduation Reggie won his first Wimbledon title, and the Doherty reign was on. Over the next several years the Dohertys between them won eight Wimbledon singles titles, and Laurie became the first foreigner ever to win the United States championship when he did so in 1903.

What did these brothers possess which permitted them to so dominate play? While they invented little in the way of stroke production, what they did do was to combine abilities in all strokes to a finished perfection which has probably been surpassed to date only by Tilden. Reggie had a flawless, smooth, seemingly effortless stroke and a marvelous sense of anticipation. He could always beat Laurie if he could pick his day, as his one weakness was a physical one brought on by chronic indigestion, making him slow of foot. Reggie, the shorter of the two, had sound strokes of a more severe nature and covered the court to perfection. They were equally at home in the back court and at net and were capable of adjusting their games to match any attack or defense they met. They were tacticians by instinct. In short, they brought the first all-court game to tennis. This overwhelming style was to be the model of many greats for years to come. To this they added the court appeal of attractive personalities combined with perfect manners and gallant sportsmanship. This made them the favorites of the large galleries which they attracted wherever they played. Thus did these remarkable brothers contribute immeasurably to the increase in popularity and technical skill of tennis.

Despite the seeming invincibility of the Dohertys, tennis marched onward at the very moment they retired; a new star rose in the person of a great natural athlete from far-off Australia named Norman E. Brookes. A self-taught, heady player, he went all the way to the Wimbledon finals on his first visit to England in 1905 before being beaten by Laurie Doherty. He never had an opportunity to avenge this defeat. However, it is interesting to note that his famous compatriot Tony Wilding, while picking Laurie Doherty as the "most graceful and finished player who ever lived," went on to say, "Brookes could beat him at his best." A lefty who relied on accurately placed shots hit with a loosely strung racket; four types of serves, each hit with the same motion; a marvelous volleying touch; classical footwork and daring shots, Brookes was truly described as a tennis wizard. He played top-flight tennis over a seventeen-year span. During this time he acquired such knowledge of the tactics and strokes of the game that the great Tilden was uneasy playing against him, even though their famous meeting was in the twilight of Brookes's career in 1920. As Tilden put it, he felt his game and brain were being picked apart by a calculating genius who eyed every move he made and then proceeded to produce an answer to each maneuver from his deep store of shots and knowledge. Brookes was a distinguished member of the all-court game school.

The reader has probably noticed that up to this point none of the tennis greats described came from the United States. We had developed a number of fine players, such as R. D. Sears, Malcolm Whitman, and William

Larned, but none had quite reached the stature of the Dohertys or Brookes. However, several American players such as O. S. Campbell, Holcombe Ward, and B. C. Wright had been experimenting with the serve and volley type of game. While it did not pay off immediately against the all-court game of the previously mentioned greats, it did contribute ultimately to the development of the game of singles. In fact, the next great champion, as if to prove the infinite variety of tennis, was an outright gambler from the Wild West who knew only one game—serve and volley.

Out of California there roared a grinning, freckle-faced, redheaded kid named Maurice E. McLoughlin. He was destined to become the first tennis hero of the man in the street. It was not just that McLoughlin was the first product of humble surroundings and public park tennis courts to become champion who appealed to the public. It was also the manner in which he achieved his victories. Whatever lingering belief still existed in the minds of the public that tennis was a pantywaist sport was swept away by the blasting racket of the California Comet. Brought up on the fast cement courts of the West, McLoughlin developed a style of brawn and speed aimed at never giving the opponent time to think. He had a lightning serve, the likes of which had never been seen before, and he followed almost every one in to the net in order to volley the return. Equipped with only these weapons plus a dogged determination, the popular McLoughlin became the world champion in the 1912–1914 period, beating both Brookes and Wilding in the Davis Cup. When at the top, the Comet won because his serve could not be broken. He seemed able to pull aces out of the hat when he needed them most. Once when down 10–11, 0–40 to Brookes in a critical Davis Cup match, he served three aces in a row and went on to win the set and match.

This serve and volley game of McLoughlin must be credited as the pioneer version of the so-called big game of today. McLoughlin was not as strong off the ground as many who followed him, so that as soon as opponents learned how to handle his serve, he was quickly dethroned. It is interesting to note that when people like Wilding and R. Norris Williams did beat McLoughlin, they managed to do so by standing in on his serve, taking it on the rise, and passing him as he came in to net. This too was the forerunner of a new style that was to lay the foundation for many memorable matches between the top servers and the ground stroke artists.

The tennis era which followed McLoughlin was one that is often termed the golden era of tennis. It was dominated by the development of the all-court game to its ultimate by William T. Tilden and William M. Johnston. For a period stretching over the years from 1915 to 1930 this remarkable pair of tennis players won between them nine U.S. singles titles, four Wimbledon championships, and twenty-nine Davis Cup Challenge Round singles matches! Never before or since has one pair so firmly, artistically, completely, and yet popularly ruled the tennis world. Johnston, a short, frail man, won the hearts of all who watched him because he possessed the fighting determination and the blasting forehand of a giant. But despite his marvelous game, Little Bill Johnston could never quite match Big Bill Tilden. They met for the U.S. title six times with Tilden winning five of the celebrated encounters.

In the minds of many students of the game, Tilden was the greatest tennis player who ever walked on a court. It is almost impossible to find a flaw in his game. He had a delivery so fast it became known as the cannonball serve. With it he whipped across aces seemingly at will at crucial points in a match. With his forehand and backhand he could play every type of spin or flat shot, using every change of angle, depth, and pace in the books to compel any opponent to play the type of game Tilden had chosen. His lob, especially his overspin variety, was deadly. He would volley with the best. He lived and breathed tennis, so that whenever a weakness showed up in his game he would practice untold hours until he conquered it completely. And he had the courage, stamina, and amazing longevity of reign of the true champion. The longevity was all the more remarkable because he was twenty-seven before he won his first U.S. title—an age when most singles players are past their peak. Finally, Tilden had that indescribable bearing of a tennis great which tends to make an opponent feel as though he does not even belong on the same court. Merely his decision to enter or not to enter a tournament created international incidents requiring the attention of kings and presidents. Truly he deserves the rating of a tennis genius, and the accolade for having contributed most to the development of tennis since the introduction of the game.

Many times Tilden delighted in playing against the strong points of an opponent just to prove he could beat him at his own game. With his amazing versatility he could outdrive a William Johnston, outchop a Wallace Johnson and even outsteady a Bitsy Grant from the base line on a clay court! At times he had streaks of tennis so devastating that those who watched still remember as if it were yesterday. Perhaps the two most celebrated such streaks were when he beat Wallace Johnson in the 1921 finals of the U.S. Nationals 6–1, 6–3, 6–1 in 45 minutes, and when he flawlessly mastered the great Manuel Alonso 6–0, 6–0, 6–2 at Forest Hills in 1923.

Defeat, the ultimate fate of all champions, finally came to Tilden through the efforts of two French masters, René Lacoste and Henri Cochet. The interesting point is that they possessed widely differing games and used quite different tactics to beat Tilden. Lacoste was a tennis machine of tremendous precision who got everything back with enough pace on the ball to keep the pressure on his opponent. Mixed in were short shots which forced Tilden to run in to net against his will. In this way he tired the aging Tilden as he waited for his opportunity to take advantage of an opening. Cochet, on the other hand, played a new dashing-and-daring type of game reminiscent of R. Norris Williams. He decided that the evolution of tennis lay in the direction of greater speed in the rallies. Thus, he took every ball on the rise or volleyed it in order to hurry Tilden on every shot and prevent him from getting set to make the type of return he wished. A favorite Cochet maneuver was to draw Tilden out of position by hitting a short, sharply angled shot, play the return for the opening created, and then take the net to volley the next one for the point. Cochet was short, graceful, and speedy. He possessed fine ground strokes hit with a short, flat swing which disguised direction up to the moment of impact. But it was his volley and half volley for which he was so well known and which, like Vincent Richards, he often hit from the middle of the court. While he was criticized for this particular tactic, it is interesting to note that his principle of playing the ball as early as possible in order to keep the opponent off balance has since been universally adopted. As earlier predicted by McLoughlin, Brookes, and Tilden, not one great champion since Cochet has played anything but the faster game with emphasis on the forecourt attack.

As we shall see, the move toward the present ultimate forecourt attack, the big game, took about twenty years. Of the celebrated Four Musketeers, Lacoste, Cochet, Jean Borotra, and Jacques Brugnon, only Borotra utilized the serve and volley game. However, the development of this attack had not quite reached the point where Borotra, with his unorthodox strokes, could conquer the all-court games of Tilden, Cochet, and Lacoste. This great French Dynasty held sway over the tennis world about seven years. It was finally broken by a lanky kid named H. Ellsworth Vines.

Vines had a brief, meteoric career as an amateur and then went on to dominate the pro ranks for five years. His game was the all-court variety built around an absolutely devastating serve hit with picturesque coordination, coupled with perhaps the most severe forehand in the history of the game. Cochet, whom Vines finally blasted right off the top of the international scene, once recorded an eloquent description of Vines's serve as follows: "No serve had the coordination of movement, vigor, and suppleness of Vines." In serving a match point at Wimbledon against Cochet, legend has it that Vines hit his flat delivery ace so hard that Cochet never saw the ball and had to await the umpire's announcement of the score to learn he had lost the match. The flat, blistering forehands of Vines were hit with the same small margin of error as his serves. Depending on his touch, and the condition of his unfortunately sensitive stomach, Vines could be merely good or just about unbeatable in his day. Certainly his fast, uncompromising game drew the admiration of the galleries and inspired many younger players.

The next dominant figure in singles was a natural, marvelously coordinated athlete—an Englishman named Fred Perry, who was also tops as a Ping-Pong player. He was noted for his running forehand, which he followed in to net to take the attacking position. Although he may not have realized it at the time, his maneuver had quite an influence on the subsequent development of the blossoming big game of the Americans. In studying Perry, they decided the only way to beat him was to take the net at every opportunity.

The player who did so was a gangling, unassuming, extremely popular, reddish-haired youngster from California named J. Donald Budge. The possessor of a powerful all-court game, Budge was noted primarily for his backhand. This shot, normally the weakest part of any tennis player's game, was a vision of smooth, overwhelming power when stroked by Budge. He made it into an attacking weapon which he utilized to become in 1938 the first player ever to win the Grand Slam—the championships of England, France, the United States, and Australia in the same year. Following this he went on to rule the professional ranks for seven years. Recognized by many as second only to Tilden among U.S. tennis greats, Budge may well be credited more in the future as having been the instigator of the transition from the all-court game to the so-called big game of today.

Against the usual opponent Budge—like his idol, Vines—just hit harder and deeper, took the net only as needed, and literally blew the victim off the court. There was no subtlety, no planning, no smart strategy—just overwhelming power. But there were times against Perry and Von Cramm when Budge had to resort to other tactics. A typical example occurred in the previously mentioned Davis Cup victory over Von Cramm. After being down 1–4 in the fifth set, Budge, with his back to the wall, changed his game and took the net at every opportunity, both on serve and return of service. His backhand return of service, which he hit on the rise as he came in, was one of the truly picture-book shots of all times. This type of power-laden net attack was the only way you could beat an inspired all-court player like Perry or Von Cramm.

Now this, as is the case with most things in tennis, was not a brand new thought. As early as 1893, James Dwight was pointing out the value of the attack when he wrote, "There is a great moral effect in being always on the offensive. If you stay back your opponent can place his stroke where he pleases, but if you go forward he has got to avoid you, and may very easily lose the stroke in trying to do so." Examples of attacking types of games have been fairly numerous from the outset. Gore, the first champion, was an attack-minded volleyer, and so were such greats as William Renshaw, O. S. Campbell, Maurice McLoughlin, and Jean Borotra. But none could match the power and perfection of the modern big game as developed through extension of Budge's game by Kramer and Gonzales.

John A. Kramer, another Californian, followed Budge as the dominant figure in tennis. At first he utilized a marvelously graceful, flawless, and powerful all-court game to sweep all before him in the amateur ranks in 1946 and 1947. He then turned professional and ruled this game another five years. It was during this time that he developed the modern game of singles, known as the big game. On a fast court it is so overwhelming that all great modern players have been forced to adopt it as a model. Benefiting from the aforementioned development of the pressing attack as contributed by Budge, Kramer went a step beyond and attacked every second. There was absolutely no compromise. Both first and second serves were followed in to the net. The power he generated, coupled with the speed, agility, reach, volley, and overhead capabilities he developed, made it practically impossible to break his service. In fact it was seldom that an opponent could win more than one point a game against his serve as placements streamed off his racket. His receiving tactics were just as unmerciful. He stood in close, took the ball on the rise, and went to the net whenever possible in order to engineer a break. All of the previous ideas of uncompromising speed were brought to a peak in his style of play, to the extent that Kramer's placements often outnumbered the sum of his nets and outs! Even the oldest of tennis critics were forced to admit that this style of play was the most devastating ever witnessed. Every ball he hit felt like a hunk of lead as it came off the ground. Without doubt, Big Jake made a lasting contribution to the development of tennis.

It seems as though it takes a Californian to beat a Californian, and the next great champion was no exception. Out of nowhere in 1948 an unranked kid named Richard A. Gonzales rocketed to the championship of the United States. After a brief two-year career at the top of the amateur ranks, he turned professional. Under the expert tutelage of Kramer, his rather spotty big game turned into a vision of annihilation even for an atomic age. Once Pancho Gonzales learned to take full advantage of his marvelous physique and natural abilities, he became unconquerable. Endowed with catlike speed with which to maneuver his athletic seventy-four-inch frame, and a real killer instinct, he was an apt pupil. By 1953 he unseated Kramer to become the top professional and remained on the throne for nine consecutive years. To accomplish this domination he utilized exclusively the big game of the Kramer school. His serve was even more powerful than Kramer's and the balance of his game almost as well-rounded, in that he could also make every shot in the books. To break his serve on a fast court was close to impossible. His speed and reflexes were so fast that he literally blanketed the net as he followed in behind every serve to volley away any returns for amazingly routine placements. Whereas many of the former champions rested in certain games and were even content to throw sets, the physical conditioning of the Kramer-Gonzales school was such that they went all out for every point without letup. This resulted in terrific pressure applied without quarter, which served to further emphasize the true quality of the big game.

Since the late 1950s the top singles notches have been dominated by the Australians. Little Ken Rosewall, a champion as a teenager, deserves recognition because of his twenty years of outstanding play and his years as top ranking professional, despite the fact he has never won Wimbledon. Roy Emerson and John Newcombe also established great records as singles players. But the best of the modern lot is Rod Laver, the lefty with a marvelous collection of unbelievable top-spin shots whose direction he hides to the last moment. He became only the second player in history, after Don Budge, to win in 1969 the Grand Slam of the English, French, U.S., and Australian singles championships. (With the advent of open tournaments in 1967, and later open Davis Cup, the need to consider the top-ranking professional as a step to greatness is no longer necessary.) The recent consistent international and professional wins of Arthur Ashe and Jimmy Connors of the United States have clearly indicated that they are well on the road to joining the company of great men singles players.

TABLE III
Outstanding Women Singles Players

	TOURNAMENT AND YEAR OF VICTORY	
NAME AND NATIONALITY	Wimbledon	United States
Blanche Bingley Hillyard (G.B.)	1886, 89, 94, 97, 99, 1900	
Lottie Dod (G.B.)	1887, 88, 91, 92, 93	
Charlotte Cooper Sterry (G.B.)	1895, 96, 98, 1901, 08	
Dorothy Douglass Chambers (G.B.)	1903, 04, 06, 10, 11, 13, 14	
May G. Sutton (U.S.)	1905, 07	1904
Hazel H. Wightman (U.S.)		1909, 10, 11, 19
Molla B. Mallory (U.S.)		1915, 16, 17, 18, 20, 21, 22, 26
Suzanne Lenglen (F.)	1919, 20, 21, 22, 23, 25	
Helen Wills Moody (U.S.)	1927, 28, 29, 30, 32, 33, 35, 38	1923, 24, 25, 27, 28, 29, 31
Helen Jacobs (U.S.)	1936	1932, 33, 34, 35
Alice Marble (U.S.)	1939	1936, 38, 39, 40
Pauline Betz (U.S.)	1946	1942, 43, 44, 46
Margaret Osborne duPont (U.S.)	1947	1948, 49, 50
A. Louise Brough (U.S.)	1948, 49, 50, 55	1947
Maureen Connolly (U.S.)	1952, 53, 54	1951, 52, 53
Maria Bueno (Brazil)	1959, 60, 64	1959, 63, 64, 66
Margaret Smith Court (A.)	1963, 65, 70	1962, 65, 68, 69, 70, 73
Billie Jean M. King (U.S.)	1966, 67, 68, 72, 73, 75	1967, 71, 72, 74

The records of the outstanding women singles players are presented in Table III. The first women's singles championship was held at Wimbledon in 1884, seven years after the inauguration of the men's tournament. The first winner was Maud Watson. Through the years this tournament has been considered the top event for women. The only other which ranks close to this one in importance is the United States championship. This tournament was begun in 1887 and was first won by Ellen F. Hansell. The play of the pioneers in the game was distinctly handicapped by the styles of the day, which required playing in hats, dresses, and petticoats. As women's dresses became shorter, the pace of their tennis increased markedly. So, incidentally, did the interest of the galleries.

The most famous women players around the turn of the century were May Sutton and Hazel H. Wightman, who did much to train youngsters and popularize the game. Wightman also stimulated international competition by presenting in 1923 the famed Wightman Cup, for which the women players of England and the United States compete each year. To celebrate the first competition, Wightman earned a point for the United States by winning her doubles match.

The next era was a golden one for women's tennis. A bombshell burst on the scene in the person of a vivacious young French girl named Suzanne Lenglen. Trained since early childhood and speedy afoot, Lenglen swept the tennis world before her with her accurately hit shots. Legend has it that she could place any of her deep or favorite soft, widely angled shots on a handkerchief. Her lively temperament was akin to that of an opera star, and wherever she played she not only attracted the galleries but also stole the headlines. Thus, she contributed mightily to bringing the women's game to the attention of the public. Many of those who followed her career thought she was the greatest of all the women players. Unfortunately she was never seen at her best by her fans in the United States, losing to Molla B. Mallory, the perennial U.S. champion, at Forest Hills in 1921.

The next great champion in this era was the complete opposite of Mlle. Lenglen. Helen Wills Moody was a serious, mechanical player who showed so little emotion that she was immediately named "Little Miss Poker Face" by the press. Behind that unruffled expression was a concentration and determination seldom seen in any tennis player. This, coupled with a depth and pace in her ground game as yet unmatched in women's tennis, carried her to the most remarkable string of victories ever won by a tennis player. From start to finish of a match she kept such a tactically well-planned and relentless pressure on her opponent that she won eight Wimbledon and seven United States championships over a fifteen-year span! Despite the fact that men tend to look down upon the game of the weaker sex, any male player the world over is willing to tip his hat to this amazing record.

Following Queen Suzanne and Queen Helen, women followed the example of the men and tended more and more to take the net and volley for the kill. Examples of this advanced technique include, first of all, Alice Marble. The possessor of a fine athletic build and natural ability, Marble was able to play the male style of forcing game as well as any woman before or since. She served and volleyed with real power and covered the court well. Her contemporaries ranked her as the best ever among the women. The next two noteworthy singles players after Marble were Pauline

Betz and Maureen Connolly. Betz was known largely for her fine back-hand and her fighting qualities; Connolly, better known as "Little Mo," after the battleship *U.S.S. Missouri,* was renowned for her solid, bombarding type of base-line driving game. (Her short stature prevented her from developing a serving, net-rushing game.)

The next group of great women players began with the highly talented, classically stroking Brazilian, Maria Bueno. Following her came those hard-hitting serve-and-volley players, Margaret Smith Court of Australia and Billie Jean M. King of the United States. Between them they dominated women's singles play for thirteen years, utilizing an aggressive game fashioned after the top men players. Chris Evert and Evonne Goolagong are knocking at the door of greatness.

In general, women play a type of singles which is a notch below that of the men, as they cannot hit as severely or cover the court as well. Thus, they have not contributed greatly to the development of the game from a technical standpoint. Instead, they tend to follow the lead of the men.

Let us now return to the most controversial portion of any tennis history—that of comparing the old-timers with the modern players. Most writers accept the better part of valor and claim that it is impossible to compare a Doherty, Whitman, Brookes, McLoughlin, Larned, Tilden, Johnston, Lacoste, Cochet, Vines, Perry, Budge, Kramer or Gonzales with a Laver. We would like to deviate from this practice of the past seventy-five years.

There is no doubt that the game of tennis, like all sports, has improved with time. The modern game, just as predicted by many former greats, is a game in which speed is king. The player must plan further ahead, think quicker, hit sooner, and move faster under greater pressure than ever before. In addition, the improved tennis rackets, balls, and clothes add to the speed of the game.

Beyond any question, the big game as played today on fast courts far outstrips the all-court game of the past. Does this mean that the more modern players, like Budge, Gonzales, Laver, Ashe, or Connors, are head and shoulders above Tilden as tennis players? We would like to answer this question in two ways. First, we believe that a Laver or an Ashe employing the big game of today would consistently beat a Tilden on grass playing his all-court game of 1920–1925. Second, we are convinced that had Tilden lived today, he likewise would have adopted and mastered the big-game style. So equipped, the Tilden of today could have murdered the Tilden of 1920–1925. There is no denying the remarkable skills of the greats of the past, but a Doherty of 1900 could provide little competition for a Doherty of today. We agree, however, that it is impossible to compare accurately a hypothetical Tilden of today with a player like Laver or Ashe.

Yes, tennis has made great forward strides since 1874. The development of the game has been entirely logical and consistent. And the best is yet to come.

3

The Game

In the first and second chapters it has been stated in various ways that tennis is an intellectual game of high order. And yet some of the top players have not been noted for their strategic powers—indeed, some have even written that they never think on the court. What is the explanation?

We have not wished or intended to frighten the beginner, the club player, or even the seasoned tournament circuit player by overemphasizing the complexities of tennis. While the game *is* truly complex, it is at the same time possible to simplify your play by developing at the outset a sound knowledge and understanding of the fundamentals. Such comprehension permits you to play the proper shot, in the most effective manner, at the right moment, almost automatically or intuitively. This is certainly what the champions do, and it explains why some evidently do not realize they are thinking while on the court. They exhibit an uncanny instinct for making the correct shot—but do not overlook the fact that this ability was developed through many hours of practice, coaching, study, and tournament experience.

There is another important part to the explanation of the seeming lack of strategic powers of some of the tennis greats. From time to time there appears on the scene a champion so outstanding that he or she just overpowers all the opposition. This was certainly the case for Helen Wills Moody and Don Budge when they were at the top of their careers—they took control of every match by just hitting so hard and so deep that they did not have to resort to brilliant tactical variations. In other words, superior stroke production minimizes the necessity for imaginative strategy. However, even in the case of a Moody or a Budge, age finally begins to have its effect on pace, and at this point you will find that these fine players depended on more study and on-court thinking to maintain their superiority.

The major purpose of this book is to provide an exposition of the funda-mentals of tennis from the standpoint of both tactics and stroke production so that the reader can learn to do the right thing at the right time. As this skill is developed, you can learn to do certain basic things essentially auto-matically in order to be able to concentrate your thinking on the more subtle factors. You will discover that this will have a tremendous effect on your ability to overcome your own weaknesses and to exploit those of your opponent.

In this chapter we will attempt to present an overall picture of the game of singles, as obtained through extensive study of actual matches, and to introduce the basic aspects of stroke production.

Before launching into details, something must be said about types of tennis courts, since this is an important consideration in determining the style of play. It may seem unbelievable, but a change in speed of bounce of a fraction of a second can and does make a big difference in the type of tennis game which should be played. Tennis courts can be ranked in terms of speed as follows: board, hard court such as cement or asphalt, grass, com-position, and, finally, clay, the slowest of all. For practical purposes, a divi-sion can be made at the point of grass, so that all matches played on grass or above can be called fast courts. Since most important tournaments are played on fast courts, the emphasis in the development of tennis has, as already shown in chapter 2, been in the direction of more and more speed. This explains to a large degree the birth of the big game. Therefore, this chapter will be devoted largely to tactics of the fast-court game, and will then deal more briefly with the slower clay-court game.

An overall examination of the game of singles indicates that the four major factors in building a sound game are:

Offense

Modern singles is definitely a game of offensive play. The offense is com-posed of serve and net play, and between them these two factors account for two thirds of all the winning shots in singles. The big serve, the hard-punched volley, and the solid overhead are the hallmarks of today's best players. This emphasis on attack is not to belittle the requirement for sound ground strokes—one must also possess these in order to be truly great.

Anticipation

Once the serve has been hit and the server follows it in to net, the struggle for the point revolves around the effectiveness of the volleys of the server and the passing shots of the receiver. Anyone who has tried to cover a 27-foot-wide tennis net against first-rate passing shots realizes the amazing speed and agility which must be developed by net players. In order to volley offensively as a net player, it is absolutely essential that you develop your anticipatory powers to a superb degree. You have to be moving in the right direction at the proper split second, or you are a goner. This means you have to know where each return is going by studying the position of the ball with respect to the player; the position of the player's feet, racket, and wrist for various shots; and the player's habits under various tactical situations.

By the same token, as the receiver, in order to have a chance to break service with your passing shots, you must be able to anticipate the moves of the net player and the depth and direction of his or her volleys. In addition, you must be able to hide your intentions to the last moment in order to fool the net player.

Concentration

To maintain the continuous application of power, speed, endurance, and tactical generalship required in top-flight singles play necessitates the utmost in concentration. In the game of today there is no place for a let-down in concentration with its consequent release of pressure on the opponent. The pendulum of play can swing rapidly against you. To convince you of the importance of this, here are just a few celebrated examples: Tony Wilding was once down to William Clothier two sets and 2–5, 15–40 in the third set, but gained a respite and won 12–10 in the fifth set. Tilden once lost to Watson Washburn when he got upset over a call while holding a lead of 6–0, 6–1, 4–4 and was about to break Washburn's serve at 30–40. Wallace Johnson was once down 1–5, 15–40 in the deciding set and made a sensational passing shot to save match point while on his knees after slipping down. This broke the concentration of his opponent and Johnson finally won 17–15. In the finals of the 1949 U.S. Championship Ted Schroeder won the first two sets from Gonzales 18–16, 6–2, but let down a bit in the third set. Big Pancho won this at 6–1 and so regained his confidence and touch that he went on to win the championship 6–2, 6–4.

So, it is well to take the advice of the great Tony Wilding, who said, "Never relax for a second no matter what the score—the body will usually respond if you have will power, pluck, and determination to spur yourself to fresh efforts."

Concentration also demands continued thought aimed at diagnosing weaknesses in the armor of your opponent's game. This entails study while watching him or her play others as well as during your own match. It is priceless information at crucial moments to know the types of shots which are most likely to draw errors from your opponents, and when you are in a hole to know the favorite shots of your opponent so that you can pull off surprising gets. All players have both weaknesses and favorite shots, so that concentration will surely reveal ways and means to pick up vital points.

Determination

Closely linked to concentration as a must in top singles players is the invaluable asset called determination. It is that hard-to-define extra in the makeup of a tennis player which permits you to lift your game at the precise moment of crisis so that you can go on to win. It is an interesting and rare quality that stamps the local as well as the national champion. Just stop and consider how often you have heard people classify players into two groups —those who will not be beaten and those who do not quite have the will to win.

Determination is a lot of things. It is not just trying hard for each point in a match. It also means the willingness to face untold hours of practicing to correct your weaknesses, the courage to come from behind, and the control of temperament and wits even under the most adverse conditions. It means developing that proper delicate balance between confidence, which is essential, and overconfidence, which is poisonous, to top performance.

TABLE IV

Fast Courts

Number and Percentile Frequency of Stroke Types During Complete Singles Matches

(Omitting Errors)

	First Service	Second Service	Return of Service	Net Shots				Base Line Shots		
				First Volley	Later Volley	Over-head	Ground Stroke	Passing	Lob	Total Strokes
No.	583	301	609	423	170	29	13	224	50	2400
%	24.5	13	25	18	7	1	0.5	9	2	

TABLE V

Fast Courts

Number and Percentile Frequency of Point-Winning Stroke Types

	First Service	Second Service	Return of Service	Net Shots				Base Line Shots		
				First Volley	Later Volley	Over-head	Ground Stroke	Passing	Lob	Total Winners
No.	202	85	180	145	112	27	13	76	23	863
%	23	10	21	17	13	3	1	9	3	

TABLE VI

FAST COURTS

Relative Probability of Winning a Point with a Given Type of Stroke Considering the Frequency of the Stroke Utilized

Stroke	Potency Factor	
Overhead	3.9	
Ground stroke at net	2.6	
Later volley	2.4	
Lob	1.9	
Passing shot	1.3	
First service	1.2	
First volley	1.2	
Return of service	1.1	
Second service	1	(basis of comparison)

Tables IV, V, and VI present an overall picture of the numbers of various types of strokes played and their relative importance in producing winners on fast courts. These data were collected from a large number of matches involving top-flight professional and amateur players. The importance of the forcing game, as shown by the frequency and lethality of net play, is worthy of note.

Let us turn our attention to play on the slower tennis courts of the composition or clay variety. Unlike doubles, which is the same game irrespective of surface, singles on a slow court is vastly different from singles on a fast court.

To prove the point, data were taken on matches involving the same players on both grass and composition courts. To nail the differences down beyond question, Pancho Gonzales and Lew Hoad were chosen for the comparison, since these expert exponents of the big game could play the same devastating game on a slow court if anyone could. However, the data, as recorded in Table VII, show a contrast in tactics which is truly striking.

Referring to Table VII, it is to be expected that the service would be more effective on the faster court, and this is shown to be the case. The really amazing difference, however, is the net play. On grass both players followed 100 percent of their serves in to the net and achieved 18 percent of the winners by putting away the first volley. On the slower composition courts they were able to follow in to net only 15 to 20 percent of their serves and to win only 2 percent of points of first volleys! The fact that later volleys produced about the same number of winners means that advances to the net were engineered largely by forcing ground strokes on the slower courts rather than via the serve. If one omits serve and return of serve, which must be played from the base line according to the rules, on grass 75 percent of all points were won at net, while on composition courts only 40 percent were won at net. Furthermore, while on grass not one single point was won with ground strokes in base line rallies, on composition courts 22 percent of all points were won in this manner with both players on the base line!

TABLE VII

Percentile Comparison of Winning Points by Gonzales and Hoad on Grass and on Composition Courts

	First Service	Second Service	Return of Service	First Volley	Later Volley	Over-head	Ground Strokes			Lob
							At Net	Passing Shot	Base Line Rally	
Grass Court	28	8	15	18	12	2	4	10	0	3
Composition Court	18	3	13	2	16	7	3	13	22	3

Percentile Comparison of Winning Points by Modern Players

	First Service	Second Service	Return of Service	First Volley	Later Volley	Over-head	At Net	Passing Shot	Base Line Rally	Lob
Grass Court	23	10	21	17	13	3	1	9	0	3
Clay Court	16	8.5	18.5	14	11.5	2	3	16.5	7	3

What all this means is that with a slower, higher bounce the defender has not only a better opportunity to reach a forcing shot, but also sufficient time to make an effective return. This gain in time of slightly less than a second means from 5 to 10 feet of court coverage, depending on whether the defender is standing or running. Such coverage blunts the weapons of the best attackers and makes it possible for a Bitsy Grant, a Manuel Orantes, or a Bjorn Borg to beat them all on clay. The ability to cover court and the possession of sound ground strokes are invaluable assets to the clay court players.

In fact, it should be remembered that the famous players listed in chapter 2 won their reputations playing the big game on grass courts, which were used for the major championships until 1975. Many of them did not possess the sound, deep ground strokes to permit them to excel on a slow court.

The differences between types of strokes which win on grass as opposed to a slow clay or composition court are clearly shown in Table VII. Even two big-game players like Gonzales and Hoad had to resort to ground strokes to win points on a composition court.

Now that clay or composition courts are being used more than grass for major championship play, we are seeing a move toward emphasis on all-court prowess. We would have to pick a different set of greats for slow-court play, contradicting some of the things said in chapter 2. Yes, for all-court prowess using depth, speed, spins, changes of pace, clever tactics, ability to keep the ball in play, court coverage, and net play behind forcing shots we would have to side with Tilden (he was dominant on any surface), Helen Wills Moody (likewise), Lacoste, Cochet, Grant, Frank Parker, Bobby Riggs, Ken Rosewall, Rod Laver (superior on any court), Billie Jean King, Margaret Court, Manuel Orantes, and oncoming Jimmy Connors and Chris Evert.

First Fundamentals of Stroke Production

Man has for many centuries used the familiar motions involved in swinging a club and throwing a rock. Swinging a tennis racket is so similar to these natural movements that anyone can play the game.

The basic fundamentals of stroke production are essentially simple motions involving body balance, weight distribution, and transfer as the stroke evolves. The payoff on a good tennis stroke, as with a good boxing punch, depends on uncoiling at the correct second just the proper amount of power of the body and throwing it behind the shot. This requires coordination of feet, knees, hips, shoulders, and arms. The degree of coordination and split-second timing achieved through long hours of practice by the top players is indeed remarkable. Just as in golf and in baseball, there is in tennis more than one way to hit a ball, but there is also a generally accepted method which most teachers use.

The first thing to consider is how to grip the racket. There are three acceptable means of gripping the racket which are identified as the eastern, western, and continental grips.

The safest and most popular grip is the eastern. It is used by most of the hard-hitting top players and recent champions. The eastern grip actually involves two grips for greater power—one for the forehand and one for the backhand and serve. These grips, as used by Tilden, Budge, Kramer, and other greats, are illustrated in figure 2. The only variations in this grip among the top players are in the spread of the fingers caused by individual hand size, racket handle size, and comfort. Notice that the face of the racket and the palm of the hand are in the same hitting plane, and there is practically no broken line at the wrist. This grip provides power, as the racket, arm, and elbow work as one piece—like an iron shaft.

The continental grip is the same for forehand and backhand. It is taken by grasping the racket as for the eastern forehand and twisting the racket about a quarter turn to the right so that the palm is virtually on top of the

forehand

Shaking hands with the racket is a good way to assume this grip, making sure the handle extends behind the heel of the hand.

backhand

Hand on top of racket with the V between thumb and forefinger pointing to the left shoulder at impact is the proper position for this grip—also used for serve. For ground strokes extend thumb back of handle for support.

Figure 2

racket and the thumb extends across the front of the handle (see figure 3). This is the grip used by such great players as Fred Perry and Rod Laver (see figure 3). It has both advantages and disadvantages. The main advantage is in volleying, since one does not have to change grips, which is most helpful in rapid volley exchanges. It is, therefore, used by many of the top doubles players. It is also effective for chop and slice strokes. However, the experts avoid teaching beginners this grip because on most ground strokes it makes greater demands on controlling the head of the racket with the wrist. This increases the margin for error and demands a strong wrist.

The western grip is taken by placing the racket flat on the ground and picking it up, or by taking the eastern forehand grip and twisting the racket about a quarter turn to the left so that the palm of the hand is behind the

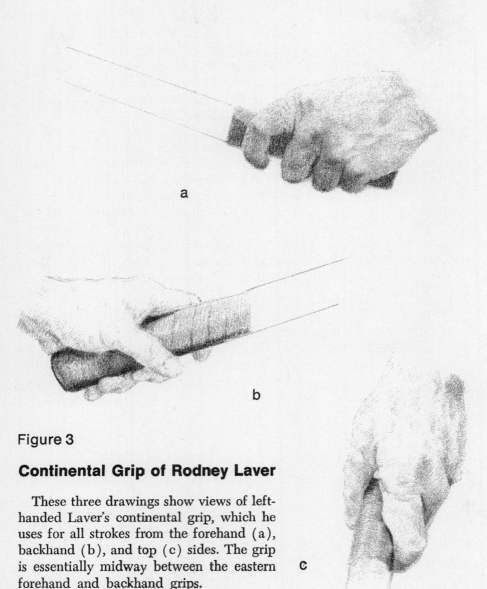

a

b

Figure 3

Continental Grip of Rodney Laver

These three drawings show views of left-handed Laver's continental grip, which he uses for all strokes from the forehand (a), backhand (b), and top (c) sides. The grip is essentially midway between the eastern forehand and backhand grips.

c

This grip demands a strong wrist and is usually not recommended for beginners. The continental grip is, however, recommended for all net play. Its particular advantage is that you can hit volleys from either sides or overhead without changing your grip, and you seldom have time to change grips in rapid-fire net play.

racket handle. This grip became popular in California, where most of the play is on hard surface courts and the ball takes a high bounce.

With all these grips the method of hitting a tennis ball can vary. There are western grip players who start the stroke with the racket head well below the ball and impart top spin to both forehand and backhand. Eastern grip specialists start the backswing high to impart some overspin. The continental grip artists hit many underspin or flat shots.

While the proper grip is important to good tennis, it is not as formalized as correct footwork and body position. Concentrate on learning proper balance while getting your racket back early, face slightly open, and hitting with a natural, relaxed baseball swing with knees bent. Remember each stroke involves four phases—anticipation, preparation, execution, and return to position. Always relax the grip between shots to avoid tiring the hand and arm.

The various strokes will be further described in connection with the chapters on serve, return of service, net play, and base line play.

4

The Serve

In this era of offensive tennis the value of the serve can hardly be overemphasized. It is the stroke which permits the striker to gain the all-important advantage of attack at the start of each point. The serve is the most frequently used stroke in championship singles, representing 37.5 percent of all strokes, as shown in Table IV in chapter 3. It also accounts for 33 percent of all winning strokes (Table V). These are really impressive numbers! However, the true importance of the serve goes well beyond even these figures. The reason for this is that the serve is also responsible in good measure for many points won later by volleying. This comes about because the serve often draws a weak return or forces the opponent out of position, thus setting the stage for a winning volley. Therefore, one can say that in championship play on a fast court the serve is directly or indirectly responsible for winning about 40 percent of all points! No wonder it is usually considered the most important single stroke.

Even on a slow court there is no doubt of the vital role of the serve. While, as would be expected, the effectiveness of the serve is reduced, it still accounts for 21 percent of winners outright (Table VII). The slower-bounding ball on a composition court also means that the service will lose some of its indirect effect, since the striker cannot often risk following his serve in to net. Now, if we allow some small number to represent indirect benefit, we can use Table VII to get a comparative value of the service on fast and slow courts. When this is done, it shows the big serves are about *twice* as effective on grass as on composition! Information of this sort is invaluable when deciding your serving tactics on a given surface. For example, expending energy banging a cannonball serve makes far more sense on grass than on a damp clay court.

Tilden has said the perfect service is 40 percent placement, 40 percent speed, and 20 percent spin. But the expert server has to possess brains as well as brawn. Not only must you be able to employ the weapons of spin, speed, and placement but, in addition, you must utilize variety and develop the capability of diagnosing the likes, dislikes, and habits of your opponent. Often the server can catch a receiver slightly out of position and slip in a shot which cannot be returned effectively, if at all. Other times the server can note on the part of the receiver a weakness against some type of spin, or a tendency under certain circumstances to take unnecessary chances, or to get careless or to let down the slightest bit. To learn and be able to take advantage of such valuable bits of information at crucial points in a match gives the server a most comforting feeling. It builds that all-important ingredient called confidence.

Fast-Court Play

The server has three major objectives: (1) to put the ball into play in a manner aimed at gaining the offense by forcing the receiver into making a weak return or moving out of position, (2) to follow in behind serve to the net position, and (3) to study the receiver while running to the net position in order to anticipate the type, speed, and direction of the return of service.

First let us consider the aim points for first serves as shown in figure 4. The preferred spots are numbered in order of priority from 1 to 3 for both courts. Some 50 percent of serves to the forehand court are aimed at area 1. The reason for this is to force the receiver out of position and wide of the court, thus opening up almost the whole court for an easy winning volley hit down the other side. (More will be said about the volley in chapter 6, Net Play.) This advantage outweighs the disadvantages of hitting to the receiver's stronger forehand side plus giving a wider angle for the return of service.

About 30 percent of serves are hit to area 2 because the backhand side is usually the weaker and the receiver will make more errors or poor returns. This is actually the case, as deep serves to area 2 draw about 40 percent errors while those to area 1 draw about 30 percent.

The final aim point, area 3, is the target about 7 percent of the time, with the rest of the court receiving the remaining 13 percent in random fashion. Area 3 is a favorite aim point when the server possesses a vicious slice delivery. The objective of the server, you will remember, is to grab the offensive. Therefore, the good player keeps moving the ball around to keep the receiver guessing and off balance. You should watch carefully to see where your opponent stands and how he or she moves, in order to take maximum advantage of any openings. For example, if the receiver moves a bit close to the center, a slice serve to aim point 3 is very effective.

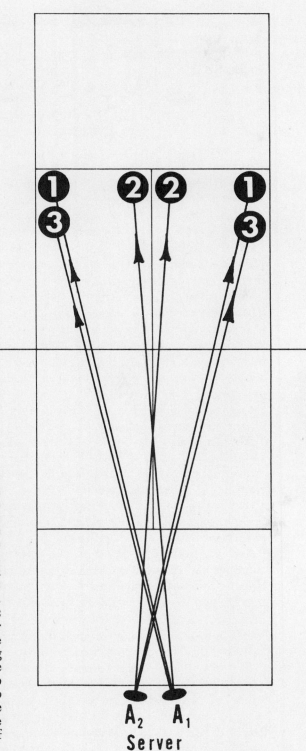

Figure 4

Aim Points for First Serves

The preferred aim points for first serves, numbered in order of preference, are shown in the diagram. Serves to the forehand court are made from A_1, and serves to the backhand court from A_2. The favorite aim point, used in at least half the cases, is deep to the outside corner. The reasoning behind this is that it forces the receiver far out of position, opening up the whole court for a winning first volley by the server. The other aim points are used to keep the receiver guessing, to capitalize on his or her stroke weakness or to take advantage of his or her being out of proper receiving position.

The favorite first serve to the backhand court is, by the same token, deep at the side line to area 1 in order to move the opponent out of position. Since this also has the added advantage of being hit to the weaker backhand side, it is used as the aim point almost habitually, actually in 56 percent of the cases. Area 2 deep on the forehand side is the target for about 30 percent of the serves to keep the receiver honest. Also, the forehand is not quite so dangerous on this side, since it will be hit from near the middle of the court, where the angle for passing the net-rushing server is a minimum. Some 10 percent of serves fall in area 3, and the remaining 4 percent are scattered around. In exceptional cases there are players like Ken Rosewall, whose forehand return of serve is less effective than the backhand. His smarter opponents exploit this fact. For example, in a match that was monitored it was found that Frank Sedgman aimed some 80 percent of his first serves against Rosewell to area 2. In another era McLoughlin always served to the center against Wilding.

The reason for placing the big serves deep (defined as within 4 feet of the service line) in the corners is readily apparent when one considers the payoff. From one third to one half of such serves are not returned, and the server ultimately wins some 70 to 77 percent of points which begin in this manner. Clearly, the big first serve is a must for top-flight singles today. The best servers get about 70 percent of first serves in, of which some 85 percent are deep. In one match we saw Gonzales get a staggering 86 percent of all first serves in when serving to the backhand court. This is what made him so hard to beat.

The aim points for second serves are quite different in order of priority, as shown in figure 5. In the forehand court some 60 percent of serves are aimed at areas 1 and 2, and about 15 percent at area 3. In the backhand court about 75 percent are aimed at areas 1 and 2, and only a sprinkling at area 3 and others. There are sound reasons for this marked preference to serve to the backhand side with the second ball. First, the backhand return of service is usually weaker. Second, and even more important, is the nature of the American twist service, the favorite type of second serve. Its rapidly spinning ball naturally kicks high to the backhand, and its medium pace gives the server maximum control and plenty of time to run well into the net position. In fact, American twist second serves hit deep to area 1 are just about as effective as fast first serves because the volleyer has time to get in closer to the net for his first volley. All young players should learn to master this simple yet most useful serve.

The important thing to stress on the second serve is to keep it deep. When the serve is deep you can win about 75 percent of the points. But when it is shallow not even a Gonzales can win better than about 50 percent of the points. Even the big-time players get only half their second serves deep, so that they are continually working to correct this defect.

Another way of emphasizing the importance of getting the first serve in

Figure 5

Aim Points for Second Serves

The preferred aim points for second serves, numbered in order of preference, are recorded. The highly favored American twist second service naturally spins the ball into the areas numbered 1 and 2 in each court. In the forehand court some 60 percent of serves by the experts fall in these areas. About 15 percent are sliced to area 3 to keep the receiver guessing, and the balance are scattered around. In the backhand court three fourths of all serves are aimed at areas 1 and 2, and the rest are split between area 3 and the rest of the court. The twist serve is employed so universally as a second serve because it provides three key advantages. First, it is easy to control, cutting down on double faults. Second, its slower speed gives the server enough time to get well into the net. And, third, its high-bounding kick to the backhand is one of the most difficult balls for the average receiver to return effectively.

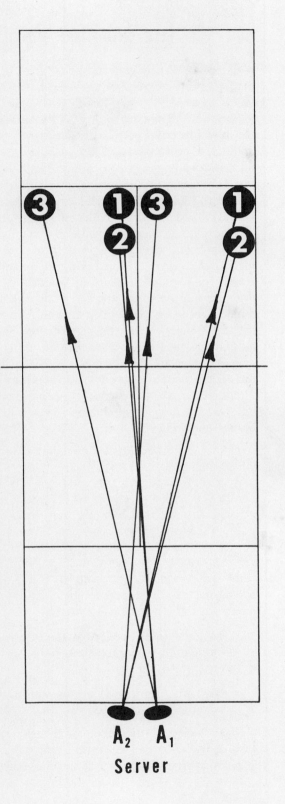

play is to note the advantage it gives the server on his first volley. In fact, the first serve gives the server a better chance to put away the first volley by a vital three-to-two ratio over the second serve.

So much for the placement of the serve in connection with carrying out the first objective of the server—that of gaining the offense. The second and third objectives call for getting into the net position and thinking and anticipating while so doing. On a fast court the modern game calls for following in behind *every* serve to the net position. (An amusing example of the importance of this was noticed in a match on grass between Gonzales and Hoad. Gonzales failed to follow serve in to net only twice in four sets. Each time he elected to remain on the base line he had a 40–0 lead and was hoping to save a bit of energy. However, in both instances his hope backfired. He lost both points and had to come in to net at 40–15 each time to win the game.) The proper path to the net varies with the type and placement of the serve and the anticipated return of service. Examples of this will be explored more thoroughly under net play. At this moment it suffices to say that you should swing your foot over the base line as you hit the service and sprint for the net. While doing so you must concentrate your attention not on the ball but on the receiver in order to anticipate the type, direction, and speed of the return of service.

Slow-Court Play

Data were collected on slow-court play at the U.S. National Clay Court Championships.

Few players possess the ability to follow serve in to the net on a slow court. You will see exceptions from time to time when a serve-and-volley artist is up against a weak opponent. But when facing an adversary equipped with a good return of service, passing shots, and lob, the net rusher will encounter real trouble. When even a Gonzales cannot follow serve in to net on a slow court, as shown in Table VII, then *you* should think twice before trying to do so. This is not to say that occasional journeys to the net represent poor tactics. On the contrary, this procedure is recommended for the following reasons:

1. To keep the opponent under pressure on the return of service by forcing him or her to watch you as well as the ball.

2. To prevent the receiver from hitting high, safe returns. By volleying away a few of these you can draw errors on the return of service, as your opponent will be compelled to keep the ball low.

The placing of the serve on the slow court is the same as that for a fast court with one exception. In serving to the forehand court most players prefer to place the first serve in the backhand corner (area 2, figure 4) about 50 percent of the time and use other parts of the court for surprise variants. The reason for this difference from fast-court play is that you have more reason to try to draw a weak return from the backhand than to try to open up the court for a winning first volley.

There are two other items to remember. The first is to keep your serves deep. This usually prevents the receiver from making the deep or sharply angled type of return which will steal the offensive away from the server. Data taken support this advice in that on deep serves the server wins points at a comfortable two-to-one ratio, while shallow serves result in a one-to-one standoff. The second is to get the first serve in as often as possible. This entails hitting the ball at somewhat less than maximum speed. The reasoning behind this suggestion is that the fast serve does not pay off on a slow court commensurate with the effort involved, while the good first serve usually keeps the receiver deep or on the defensive and saves the server valuable energy, as well as cutting down on double faults.

The Service Strokes

There are three principal types of service—the cannonball or flat service, the slice, and the American twist—and the same basic rules of stance and delivery apply to each. Their variation lies in how the racket head strikes across or into the ball and in the follow-through to left or right. The service grip is the same as that used for the eastern backhand, with the racket handle held firmly but not too tightly.

More than any other stroke, the serve accents the importance of the throwing arm, since the shot cannot be hit properly unless the racket meets the ball at the top of the throw. The fastest serve is not always the best, so it is wise to develop control first and to learn to mix up your delivery with changes of pace and spin.

To get the slice service, the ball is tossed so it is struck slightly to the right of the head with the racket following through across the body with your arm not quite fully extended. This imparts a rolling top spin to the ball so that it bounces away from the opponent toward his or her forehand side. To get the flat service the ball is tossed not quite so far to the right and the ball is hit with a flat or open face with the follow-through ending on the left side (see figure 6). With the American twist serve the ball is tossed overhead and slightly to the left and hit with a snap of the wrist as the arm moves directly from left to right with the follow-through finishing on the right side. This imparts a spin to the ball so that it bounces high toward the opponent's backhand.

Actually, the top servers learn to hit all three varieties of serves with essentially the same toss in order to avoid telegraphing to their opponent the type of service about to be delivered.

The service requires the coordination of two separate activities aimed at bringing the ball and racket into perfect union at the top of the swing. First, you should take a position within 4 or 5 feet of the center of the base line, allowing you to hit down the middle or angle the serve cross court. The left foot, pointing at a 45-degree angle toward the base line, should be 2 or 3 inches behind it to avoid the possibility of a foot fault, and the right foot about 18 inches behind the left. The weight is evenly distributed between the two. The racket is tilted upward at a slight angle, the throat cradled gently in the fingers of the left hand. The ball should be held comfortably in the fingers, not the palm. Relaxation and balance are the most important keys to the stance at this particular moment.

The stroke begins with both arms commencing their separate actions simultaneously.

The right arm moves down and back like a pendulum, the wrist remaining in a natural uncocked position until the racket is overhead and behind the back. When your elbow has reached the height of your shoulder in this continuous circular backswing, the wrist is broken and the racket head drops. There are variations in the length of the backswing. Some players arch the back and drop the racket head way down until it "scratches the back," while others have shortened the backswing. The important thing to remember is to have the shoulder, arm, and racket in a pitcher's about-to-throw position before starting the forward motion. As the forward thrust begins, the wrist snaps the racket head forward and you achieve the feel of "throwing" the racket—just as if it were a baseball—across the net into the service court. The follow-through is natural, with the weight shifting entirely to the left foot. Many players draw the right foot closer to the left foot just before hitting the ball. At impact the left knee is slightly bent. Once the ball is struck, the right foot follows across the base line in the direction the ball is taking so that your weight is behind the shot and you are ready to start your sprint to the net or take the anticipatory position at the base line from which you are ready to begin the next stroke.

At the same time, the left hand has thrown the ball—in a natural, easy motion—to a point where the racket will meet it at the absolute top of the toss—the ball neither rising nor falling at the point of impact. The toss should leave the hand fairly high, with the left arm continuing up until it is fully extended, thus improving accuracy by limiting the distance the ball must travel to reach its peak. Intensive practice is required to achieve a correct toss, but it will pay off, as defective tosses, particularly low tosses, are responsible for many faults and poor serves.

If you find your serve is hitting the net or is too shallow, lift your sights by hitting "out" at the ball. And if your serves are going too deep, bring them back into the court by lessening the speed of the serve and increasing the spin on the ball. Spin lends control—even a server of the highest caliber seldom serves a truly flat ball in an entire match.

Figure 6

Ashe's Flat (Cannonball) Serve

Arthur Ashe, despite the fact that he does not possess a rugged, muscular build, has one of the fastest serves of the current tennis greats through the exercise of great body and wrist action and timing.

Ashe is standing in perfect position, with left foot 45 degrees to the base line and feet about 12 to 15 inches apart, as he starts the racket down and begins his toss with the left hand. His weight is slightly on his right foot.

a

The racket is now at the bottom of the swing back as the tossing arm continues upward. The weight is starting to shift forward, and the left knee is bent slightly.

The ball has been released as the left arm is now straight and the racket head is waist high. The left knee is bending more while the weight shifts almost entirely to that side.

As the racket arm continues upward and the wrist starts to cock, the weight is now essentially all on the ball of the left foot as the right foot is brought forward with the toe on the ground. Both knees are bent. The shoulders are turned perpendicular to the net.

e

The racket arm is now approaching the completion of the backswing. At the completion Ashe's elbow will be pointed upward, the racket straight down and the back slightly arched, as in the slice and American twist serves. His body is now leaning well into the court, the knees are straightening to push off and gain height and all the weight is on the left foot. The left hand has come down to clear the hitting zone and help maintain balance.

Ashe has just completed contact with the ball and has broken his wrist straight downward on the flight path of the ball, as is characteristic of the flat serve. His legs, body and racket arm are in an extended straight line in

f

the same fashion employed by Tilden and other great servers. The shoulders have turned straight toward the net to add power. The left hand is brought in to help balance against the forward motion of the racket arm. Note particularly the feet. The current foot-fault rule allows both feet to leave the ground as long as neither one touches inside the base line prior to striking the ball. Ashe has taken every advantage of this rule by pushing with his left foot as the right foot comes over the line so that his right foot is almost a step into the court when the ball is struck. This gains him an important split second in his run to the net position.

g

h

Ashe's right foot has not quite touched the ground as his run to the net
begins. The follow-through after the snap of the wrist is continuing, and the
racket face is almost flat with respect to the receiver in the forehand court.
The racket arm is fully extended, and the left hand is tucked in to the chest
to help the balance.

Ashe is completing his second step in the court as he races with body still
bent forward from the tremendous follow-through of his flat service stroke.
His eyes are on his opponent to try to anticipate the type of return.

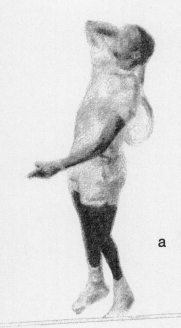

a

Figure 7

Ashe's Slice Serve

The backswing is standard as the elbow points up and the racket head is straight down at the completion. The back is slightly arched.

As the racket head moves up it is pointing almost straight back while Ashe turns his body and shoulders toward the net. This form coupled with the toss of the ball a bit to the right and about 10 inches in front of the head is the telltale signal of the slice service for which the alert receiver must watch.

b

c

d

At close to the moment of impact you can see from the position of the racket that Ashe is about to slice (hit around, down, and over the ball). Note that he is almost facing the net and is hitting the ball over his right shoulder.

At the finish Ashe's racket is still in the slice position in front of his right leg. This ball landed in the forehand corner of his opponent's service court, and the strong spin caused it to curve about 5 feet off the court beyond the sideline after the bounce.

5

The Return of Service

There is no doubt that one of the most difficult strokes to execute both well and consistently is the return of service. Substantiation for this statement is not difficult when you consider that about 25 percent of serves are not returned at all (see Table VIII), that service is broken only about one in five times, and that the return of service enjoys a low potency (see Table VI in chapter 3). The vital importance of developing a reliable return of service is, therefore, obvious. This is the weapon with which service breaks are engineered. It is the stroke that sets the offensive and defensive tactics for each point.

TABLE VIII		
SERVES NOT RETURNED		
Ranking Professionals and Amateurs		
Surface	*1st Serve*	*2nd Serve*
Grass	35%	25%
Clay	25%	22%

The receiver should have in mind five major objectives:
1. Assume the most advantageous receiving position.
2. Anticipate the type of serve to be delivered.
3. Return the ball at all costs.
4. Force the server into making a defensive return.
5. Move in to the net at the earliest possible opportunity.

The reasoning behind these rules will become evident as this chapter unfolds. The logical way to begin is to analyze the starting position.

The proper position for the receiver can be determined quite accurately by means of rather simple logic. Strangely enough, this logic is not well understood by many players, even those of the ranking variety. If you will just master the factors behind good position play, you will win a lot of points as a receiver. So, let's proceed to get these clearly in mind.

The best way to describe receiver position play is by means of diagrams. The factors which the receiver must consider are the position of the server, the speed and spin of the service, the tactical situation, and his own capabilities with respect to anticipation, speed, and stroke production. These factors are explained briefly in figures 8, 9, and 10.

There has been a rather steady trend forward in the case of the position of the receiver. Back in 1886 Dr. James Dwight, father of American lawn tennis, stood well back of the base line to receive service. In the twenties Tilden was receiving at about 3 feet back of the base line. Borotra and Johnston stood on the base line. Then certain players such as R. Norris Williams and Henri Cochet began moving in until they were about 3 feet inside the base line. This development has been generally adopted as the soundest procedure by the top players of today. They move inside the base line as far as they dare, depending on the server. This is the proper counter to the serve-and-volley big game for the following reasons: (1) The earlier you return the service the sooner the server must hit his volley. (2) The earlier you hit the ball the easier it is to cover court, as the combined spin and speed of the serve has less opportunity to pull you wide of the court. In addition, you can make a better offensive stroke from the standpoint of both speed and angle from close in. (3) When the chance presents itself, it is easier for you to get in to the net as you are already a step or two on your way.

For many of these same reasons, and those covered in figures 8, 9, and 10, it is also recommended that the beginner and club player practice standing in to receive the serve and taking the ball on the rise. This is desirable whether playing on a fast or a slow court. In effect it gives you a better chance of taking the offense, whether the server rushes the net or remains on the base line. This is, of course, especially true in the case of the second service. Anyone who has ever watched the amazing little Rod Laver run in and around a twisting second serve off the racket of big John Newcombe knows what we mean. He moves in to within 6 to 10 feet of the service line and powders the return of service with his forehand for many telling winners. This has a very upsetting effect on the server and teases him into double faulting. While you may not be a Laver, you are probably not facing the serve of a Newcombe. So you can do the same at your own level of play, whatever that might be.

The major reason why a Laver can accomplish this is directly related to our second objective, *the ability to anticipate*. The importance of this ability can hardly be overemphasized. You gain this tremendous advantage only by careful study of your opponent. A particular player is usually capable of serving better to the right or left. And most players telegraph the direction of the serve by the way they toss the ball and make the service stroke. For example, most players toss a bit to their right and in front for a slice serve, and swing across the body; toss straight and in front for a flat serve; and toss behind the head and swing away from the body along the base line for an American twist serve. Many have certain habits or favorite serves under certain tactical situations which further permit you to diagnose intentions. For these reasons you must study your opponent very carefully, during other matches and during warmups and play against you.

Lest you think this is poppycock, the matter of small but giveaway habits is not unusual even among tennis greats. Don Budge once revealed to Bobby Riggs that he always knew, because of a certain mannerism, when Riggs was about to try for an ace. Riggs immediately indicated his disbelief. So Budge explained that ordinarily Riggs served with his racket head high and his wrist cocked upward, but when he wanted to serve hard, he lowered his wrist position in a telltale fashion which permitted Budge to get ready for a fast delivery. Riggs said, "I still don't believe it!" Quickly they found a racket to test the point. Just as Riggs started through the motions of a hard serve he turned toward a smiling Budge and cried out an incredulous, "Well, I'll be damned—you're right."

Of course, another means of anticipation is to know your own weaknesses, as your opponent will almost certainly serve to take advantage of them. For example, people usually served to the forehand of Frank Parker and Ken Rosewall and to the backhand of Frank Shields.

Now to return to the receiver's third and most basic objective: to *get the ball back*. The experienced player as well as the beginner should concentrate on achieving success in this department. After all, you can't win if you don't return the ball, and often even the saddest and feeblest of returns will draw an error from an overanxious opponent. In addition, by returning everything in sight you exert relentless pressure on the server. Many a server has become unsettled and has finally broken by being forced to win every point the hard way.

There is one fact about return of service that should be engraved indelibly upon the racket handle of every player as a constant reminder. Data taken on five hundred points in many matches indicate clearly that the receiver has almost an even chance of winning each point, once he or she has successfully returned the service. So practice getting the return back consistently by any means possible—you will find it will pay off handsomely. To do so you must, above all else, keep your eye on the ball.

Figure 8

Position of Receiver
First Lesson: Direction of the Serve

Referring to the backhand court:

One objective of the receiver is to cover the court. In order to be able to reach serves hit to right or left, the receiver must be near the center of the area to which it is possible to direct serves. As a first step in determining proper position, you should note the point from which the server will make the delivery. You should then imagine a point M in the center of the service court, and take your position near the base line on a straight line drawn from the server through point M. For example, if the server stands at A_2, the receiver should stand near F_2, and if the server is at A_3, the receiver should move over to F_3. Some players stand a little to the right or left of the center line if they find their reach or stroke production is better from one side or the other.

Referring to the forehand court:

The straight, flat serve can be delivered only in the area defined by B_2 and B_3. There-fore, the proper receiving position is, as just described, at the midpoint F_1. But this receiving position must be altered if the server imparts spin to the ball. A good slice serve curves to the right and can draw the receiver as much as 10 feet off the court to point B_4, and a twist serve can pull the receiver to left a few feet to point B_1. Therefore, depending on the type of serve you face, you may be forced to modify your starting position to the right or left of the middle line A_1-M-F_1. In other words, you have to take a position midway between the limits of the *serving area capability* of the particular server opposing you. Thus, you might have to move your initial position from F_1 to midway point C and be prepared to move to the right or left as you note from the server's toss the type of serve that will be delivered. This is why knowledge by the receiver of the server's capabilities and anticipation of the server's intentions are so important.

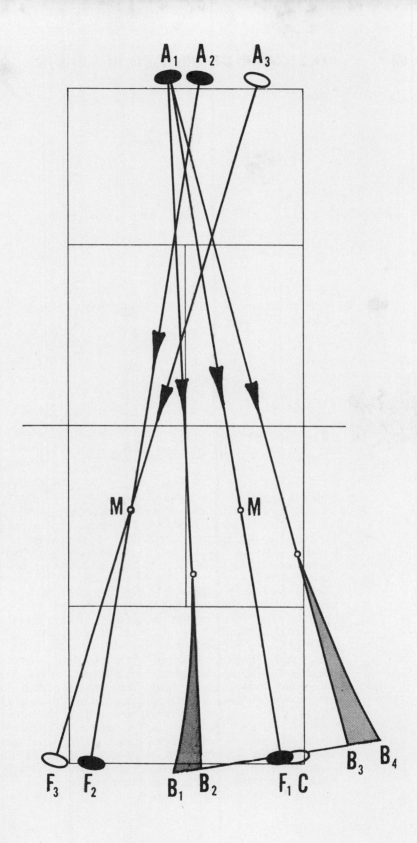

Figure 9

Position of Receiver
Second Lesson: Speed of the Serve

The next thing the receiver must take into consideration is the speed of the serve. Since this becomes more important as the speed of the serve increases, let us take as an example a serve traveling at 90 miles per hour (the best ones exceed 100 mph). Such a serve travels the length of the tennis court in just six tenths of a second!

When you analyze carefully such factors as the speed and path of the ball and the reaction time, speed, and reach of the player, you find there is an area the receiver cannot cover (see shaded portion). This is true unless the receiver anticipates the intentions of the server and gets an explosive start in the proper direction. Note carefully that the deeper you stand the *less* able you are to cover the rapidly widening and curving area open to the serve. For this reason, modern players usually receive near B_1 rather than behind the base line at B_2 as did many of the old-timers.

The closer in you stand along the line B_2-C, the better able you are to get your racket on the serve. But if you move in too close, you are faced with a more difficult shot because of the lower bounce on the ball. Thus, the general rule is to receive one to three feet inside the base line (B_1), or as far in as your style and talent permit against the server you are opposing.

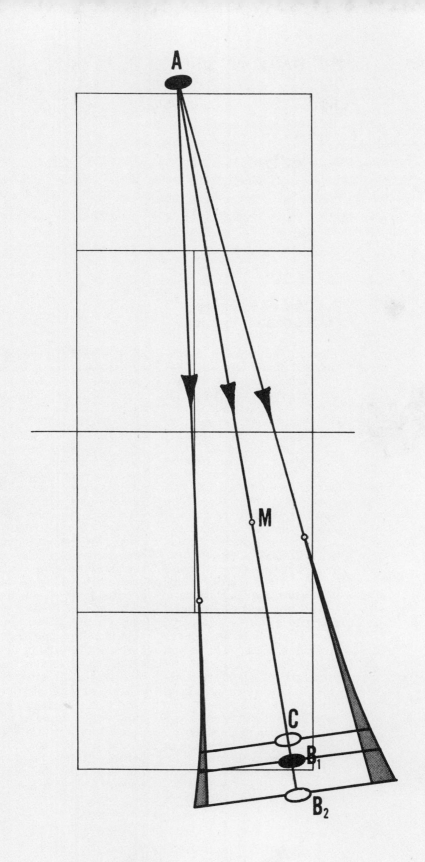

Figure 10

Position of Receiver
Final Lesson: Tactics

Taking into account all factors, this figure shows the recommended positions for receiving first serves (forehand court) and second serves (backhand court). The areas are purposely left somewhat flexible, as the receiver must judge the particular situation.

The general conclusions drawn from figures 8 and 9 are to receive on a line bisecting the serving area capability, and as far inside the base line as possible consistent with good stroke production. Consideration of sound tactics for the receiver tends to fortify these conclusions.

Against a net-rushing server you gain a double advantage by standing as far forward as possible in area B_1. First, you have a better chance of returning the ball at the vulnerable feet of the server, as you provide less time to run in to the net; and, second, you have a wider angle open for the passing shot by virtue of being closer to the net.

On the second service the receiver can take more chances and move in still closer in the B_2 area. This is because most second serves are of the slower American twist variety and tend to be more shallow as the server can ill afford the chance of a double fault. This will often allow you to take the offense away from the server by making a forcing return, and sometimes even permit you to take the net, particularly if the server stays back.

Finally, you have to keep working to determine just where to receive service to best advantage. This means you must develop your ability to anticipate the server's intentions; to learn how to take the ball on the rise; to make quick starts; to learn how to adjust your receiving position depending on your ability to move and reach to the right and left; and the relative strength of your forehand and backhand; and to know when to take chances or tease the server into errors. Remember in selecting receiving position that inches can make the difference between won and lost points.

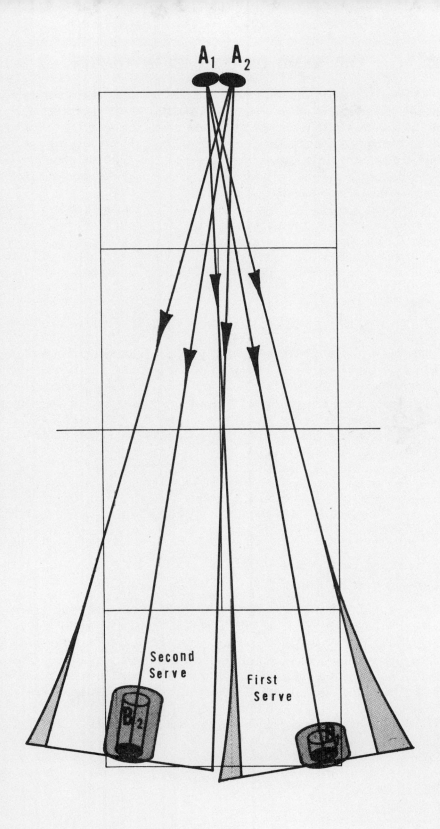

To give you a comparative measure so you can rate your performance, the top players return about seven out of ten first serves and second serves on fast courts. On slow courts they return about seven and a half out of ten first serves, and eight out of ten second serves. The better performance on the slow court is not due entirely to the slower, and truer, bounce. The receiver can usually play a safer return, higher and deeper, because the server is less likely to take the net.

Now it is time to turn our attention to the fourth objective of the receiver: to *force the server into making a defensive shot* so that the receiver can take command. The techniques to accomplish this will have to be considered in two parts—the shots to make, first, when the server rushes the net and, second, when the server remains on the base line.

Return of Service When Server Rushes the Net

There are two major points to keep in mind in returning serve against the player who follows serve in to net. These are (1) to take the ball as early as possible and keep the return low so that the server will not have time to get on top of the net and will be forced to volley up defensively, and (2) to keep the server guessing by mixing up cross-court and down-the-line drives, dinks, and occasional lobs. Avoid hitting to the middle.

The aim points used by the experts for return of service against the net rusher vary with the location from which the shot must be played. A great deal of information was collected on this subject during many tournament matches—on both grass and clay courts—involving the top players of the world. To provide some guidelines, let us take a look at figures 11, 12, 13, and 14.

Return of Service When Server Remains on Base Line

Only a handful of players in the world have a sufficiently powerful service to permit them to play the big game and follow every service in to the net. And even these international experts can ill afford to do so when playing on slow courts. Therefore, the great majority of readers will ordinarily return service against an opponent standing near the middle of the base line. This calls for tactics and shots which are completely different from those just described. For this reason, it is imperative that the receiver develop the habit of noting first before executing a return whether the server is moving in to the net or remaining on the base line. Some types of returns which would be excellent against the base line player can be murdered if the server catches you off your guard and rushes the net; the reverse is also true.

Figure 11

Aim Points for Return of Deep Service Against Net-Rushing Server

On first and second serves hit deep to area 1 in the forehand court, the experts return some 40 percent cross court to area 6, 40 percent to the middle (area 7), and 20 percent down the line to area 4 or 5. Most returns from deep serves are drives or slices with the dink used as a variant from time to time. As far as outright winners on the return are concerned, the cross-court and down-the-line shots hit from area 1 are about equally decisive. However, from area 3 the cross-court return to area 6 gives more outright winners. Most returns from area 2 are hit back to area 7. On the matter of overall won and lost, the cross-court and down-the-line returns are almost equally effective—about 55 percent of successful returns to these areas resulting in points won. Of returns to the middle (area 7), only 40 percent result in points won.

This means that on deep serves to the forehand court the receiver should try to direct the return down the line or cross court as shown in the diagram. Either one forces the advancing server to run farther and reach for the volley, thus provoking errors or weak volleys which present the receiver with opportunities to make successful passing shots. On the other hand, the return to the middle can usually be volleyed by the server less hurriedly and more effectively.

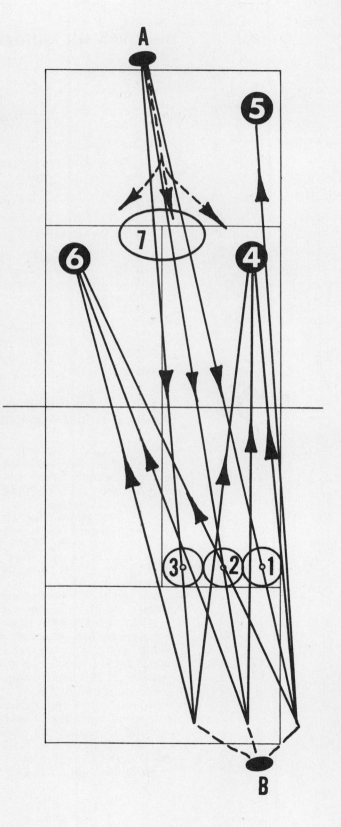

Figure 12

Aim Points for Return of Shallow
Service Against Net-Rushing Server

On first and second serves hit shallow to the forehand court the experts favor the down-the-line return. Approximately 50 percent of returns are hit down the line to areas 4 and 5, and 25 percent each to areas 6 and 7. These returns are usually forehand drives or slices with an occasional dink mixed in.

Most outright winners are produced by down-the-line returns from area 1 and cross-court returns from area 3. On overall won and lost, the down-the-line returns from areas 1 and 2 to areas 4 and 5 are certainly to be favored. From area 3 the cross-court return is more effective. These successful returns to the side lines win points in about 60 percent of the cases. However, returns to the middle (area 7)

should be avoided, as they lose more points than they win.

The receiver should learn to take advantage of a shallow serve by moving well in on the ball and hitting it crisply down the line, mixing in sufficient cross-court returns to keep the server guessing. Note the cross-court return can be more sharply angled when hit from a position closer to the net. Since these tactics will catch the net-rushing server back at a poor volleying position near the service line, the receiver should be able to win about two thirds of such points. But do not forget, you have to make the return. On sighting the opening, do not become overanxious and make an error.

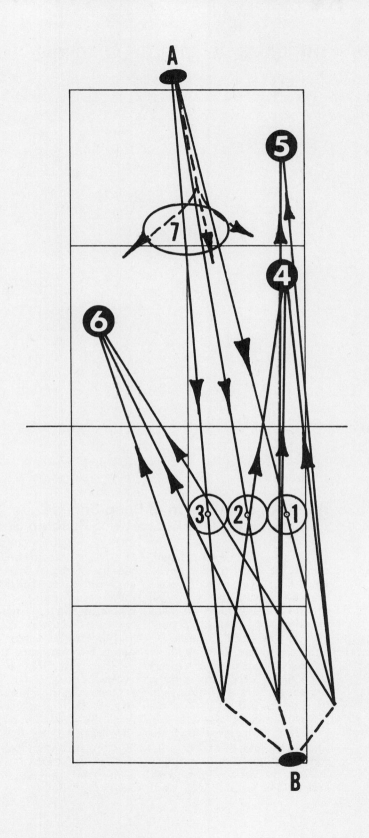

Figure 13

Aim Points for Return of Deep Service to Backhand Court Against Net-Rushing Server

On the first and second serves hit deep to the backhand court, the experts favor the cross-court return. Approximately 60 percent are hit cross court to area 6, 25 percent to the middle (area 7) and 15 percent down the line to areas 4 and 5. The returns from deep serves are usually drives or slices with the dink used occasionally.

Most outright winners are produced by cross-court returns from areas 1 and 3, with some coming from down-the-line shots, particularly from area 1. On overall won and lost, the cross-court and down-the-line returns are equally effective. Successful returns to these areas result in winning points in about 57 percent of the cases. However, returns to the middle (area 7) win points only one time in three, so that this area is to be avoided.

Once again, this demonstrates that returns which force the server to run farther and reach for the ball result in more errors and less decisive volleys. Obviously, this is the tactic for the smart receiver to follow.

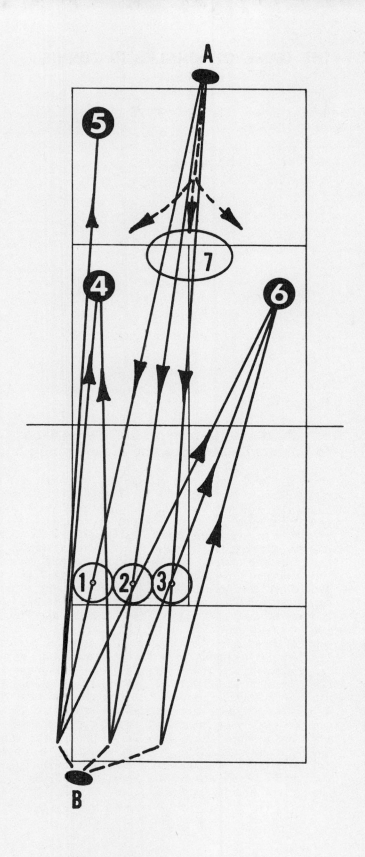

Figure 14

Aim Points for Return of Shallow Service to Backhand Court Against Net-Rushing Server

On first and second serves hit shallow to the backhand court the experts favor the cross-court return. Few serves ever land in area 3. Approximately 50 percent of returns from areas 1 and 2 are hit cross court to area 6, 25 percent down the line to areas 4 and 5, and 25 percent to the middle area (area 7). In contrast to returns from shallow services from the forehand court, the majority of returns from shallow serves hit wide to the backhand court are sharply angled dink shots. When the receiver gets in position fast enough to make the down-the-line return, it is usually a drive or slice.

Most outright winners are produced by the faster down-the-line return to areas 4 and 5. The pros often take the net behind a sharply angled dink return from area 1 and try to put away the return volley (see figure 19 in chapter 6). Returns to either side line result in winning points—about two thirds of the time. On the other hand, returns to the middle result in losing points about two thirds of the time.

The receiver should learn to take advantage of the shallow serve by moving forward into position rapidly in order to be able to take the ball early and drive or sharply angle it past the net-rushing server before he or she is past the vicinity of the service line. Such tactics should pay handsome returns.

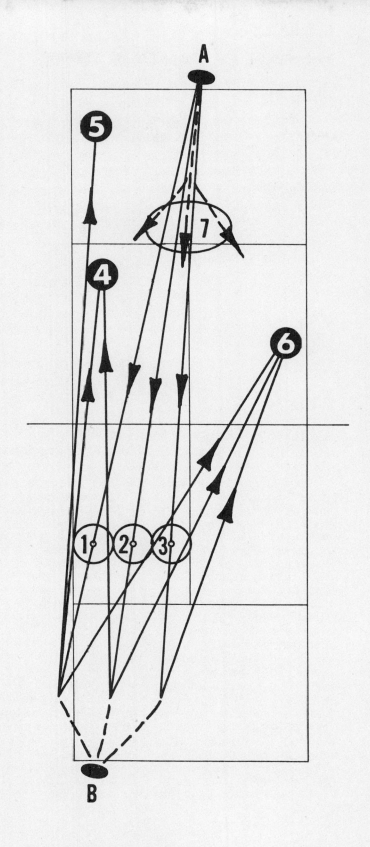

Figure 15

Composite Picture of the Best Areas for Return of Service Against Net-Rushing Server

This diagram is one which should be stamped indelibly on the receiver's brain. It presents a summary picture of the best aim points for the return of service. This is the pattern which makes possible the engineering of the all-important service break.

The most lethal shots, which usually result in outright winners, are down-the-line or cross-court returns landing in the heavily shaded areas. Note that the down-the-line and cross-court areas overlap somewhat. These heavier-shaded areas are recommended, as they force the volleyer to run far and to reach off balance in striving to play the ball. Thus any return the server is able to execute will usually leave him

or her open to be passed on the succeeding shot.

The lighter-shaded portion in the middle, while much less lethal in producing outright winners, will often force an error or weak return if the serve can be taken early and the return made quickly enough to catch the server at the service line. Returns here at the feet of the volleyer make him or her volley up or attempt a difficult half volley.

Avoid the danger area whenever possible since this is the area in which the volleyer operates with greatest effectiveness—winning two out of three points. Returns to the shaded areas shift the odds in your favor—the receiver wins 60 percent of points after returns of service to these areas.

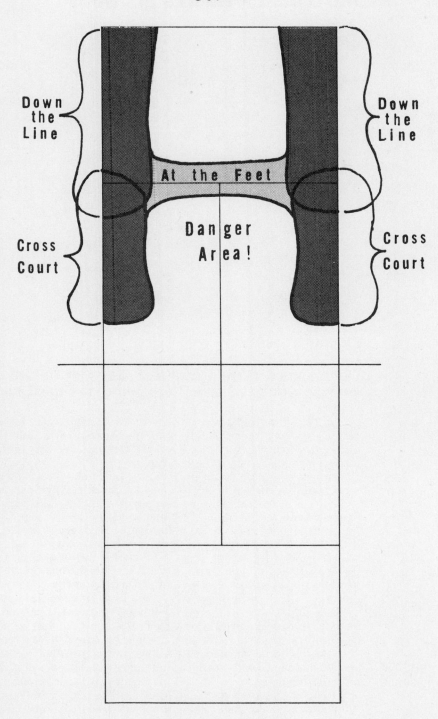

Figure 16

Composite Picture of the Best Areas for Return of Service Against Server Remaining on Base Line

The best aim points for return of service are completely different when the server remains on the base line. This is the situation usually faced by most receivers the world over.

Above all, keep the return deep—that is, within about 10 feet of the base line. If you do just that you should win at least 50 percent of the points after such returns. While cross-court or down-the-line returns to the corner areas A and C are preferred in order to run the server, any deep return to areas A, B, or C is acceptable, particularly in the darker-shaded portion near the base line.

If the serve is shallow, it is sometimes advantageous to hit a sharp cross-court return to area D or E. Such returns can result in outright winners or run the server so far off the court that his or her return can be put away.

By far the best tactic against most players without national ranking is to hammer away at the backhand by returning the great majority of serves to areas C and E. This takes advantage of the weaker side and sets the stage to outmaneuver the opponent.

By way of contrast, any returns of service to the danger area result in lost points about two out of every three times. A shallow shot in base line play usually opens up the floodgates in favor of the opponent. The drop shot should be used sparingly, and then only after faking a drive from a shallow service.

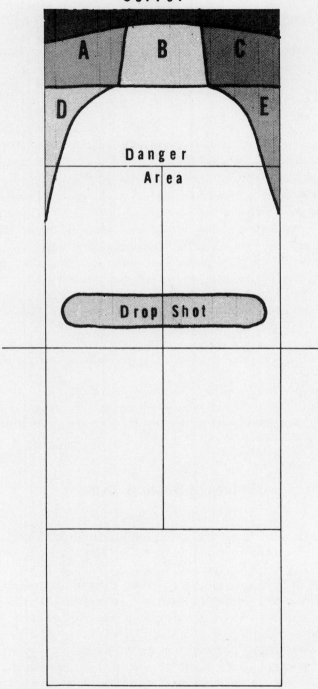

When the server remains back, the return of the serve must be kept deep—within 10 feet of the base line—to be effective. There is no sense in trying to keep the return so low that it is in danger of hitting the net —a mistake made by many weekend players. Instead, the shot should be played one or more feet above the net as a flat, top-spin, chop, or sliced drive. Even high, soft shots (half lobs) which land near the base line are acceptable. The deep ball pins the server to the base line and often causes a shallow return which allows the receiver to take the offensive by hitting a forcing shot and taking the net. On the other hand, a shallow return, with few exceptions, hands the server the all-important advantage of taking the offense. To drive home the importance of this advice, remember the shallow return usually loses two out of three times, whereas the deep return gives the receiver a better than even chance of winning the point. The details of the proper aim points are shown in figure 16. Note the emphasis on returning service to the weaker backhand side.

If the server loses a lot of points as a result of high, deep returns, he or she will probably try an occasional trip to the net. Since such high returns are easily volleyed, remember to watch and be prepared to shift to the low, spinning return of service tactics shown in figures 11, 12, 13, and 14. Such returns, you will find, are much easier to make from the slower, higher-bounding serve encountered on a slow court. Indeed, this is the reason even the best servers have trouble trying to rush the net on clay or composition courts.

Once you have mastered the different types of returns of service against various servers, you will find you have a good chance to break service. But to do so, you must be ever alert to the changing tactics of the server.

Return of Service Strokes

The methods used in executing the forehand and backhand drives and the lob will be covered in chapter 7, Base Line Play. As has been mentioned, these are among the accepted and valued methods of service return, and we do not wish to detract in any way from their importance by failure to describe them in this section. In fact, the major objective in service return is to get the ball back any way you can in order to capitalize on possible errors on the part of the server. If one type of service return stroke is not working for you, always have others in reserve to try.

The particular types of strokes to be described in this section are a family of shots which have come to be used specially for service returns against net-rushing servers. Most of these involve spin to develop control and to keep the ball low and slowly paced. This gives the volleyer three problems

—he or she has to volley a spinning ball, he or she must volley up, and the slow ball takes the sting out of the return. Meantime, the slow return gives you time to move into position for the shot.

The returns of the spinning type include the chop or chip, slice, and dink. The chop is started with the racket head at about shoulder level with face open; the forward motion of the stroke is down under the ball to give it underspin. The ball can be angled sharply or hit down the line by adjusting the position of the racket at moment of impact and the direction of the follow-through, which is shorter than for the drive. The slice is usually used to impart spin to a low ball. The racket actually slices under and across the ball from right to left on the forehand and left to right on the backhand, giving the ball a nasty sideways-bouncing motion. Dink is the term used for either type of spin shot when it is hit very softly, often at wide angles, just over the net. All these shots are made easiest when the player utilizes the continental grip because of the flexible wrist action required in making the strokes.

6

Net Play

There is no way more convincing to illustrate the revolution in top-flight tennis than to recall that as recently as 1928 the great Tilden was still winning matches without making a single volley. Even calculating tacticians like Lacoste were just beginning to observe that "more and more the volley appears to be an indispensable stroke." Today the revolution is complete. In championship singles on fast courts hardly a point is played without at least one player camped at net in the volleying position. There is no doubt that the young player must now learn to be equally at home with the volley and overhead as with any other stroke.

This revolution is as sound as it is complete. The net position is the offensive position in tennis, and the volley and overhead are the knockout blows. The tactical pattern is to set the stage for a net stroke and then employ it for the kill. These contentions are borne out by the figures in Tables V, VI and VII in chapter 3, which show that the most lethal strokes, as well as a high percentage of all winners, are produced at the net, particularly on fast courts. The fact is that the top players punch or smash away from the net area one fourth to one third of all points won.

The aforementioned tactical requirement of setting the stage warrants emphasis. The volley might well be thought of as two consecutive strokes, the first involving an approach shot and the second the volley. For the volley to be a winner, the approach shot must be effective. The greatest weakness of many young players is a tendency to go to the net behind a serve or ground stroke which is insufficient to set the stage for a winning volley. This usually results in a lost point, as the opponent is presented with the opportunity to counter with passing shots. It is much like a boxing combination—you can seldom lead with the right; instead, you have to set the opponent up by knocking him off balance with the left before you can rock him with your right. Practice in developing good forcing approach shots which will drive the opponent off balance is an essential part of the modern volleying game which is all too often overlooked.

Many weekend players seem to be afraid to venture into the net area. They do not feel at home up forward, nor do they appear to know what to do once there. Before this chapter is completed we hope we will have convinced the reader that net play not only is vital to the molding of a winning game but also is easy to learn and adds a lot of fun to tennis.

Perhaps a simple example will help to show that the volley is not just a weapon for the expert with the big game but is also of tremendous value to the average player or beginner. Figure 17 illustrates a type of point the reader will surely recall having played many times. It reveals clearly the value of using the volley for the kill.

Net play provides two major advantages. First, it allows you to capitalize on a good approach shot or a weak return. Second, it gives you the incalculable advantage of being on the attack, with all the pressures upon the opponent which this involves.

To become a good net player it is necessary to learn the following: (1) how to get to the net, (2) proper volleying positions and anticipation of the opponent's return, (3) proper placing of volleys and overheads, and (4) the techniques of the net strokes. These factors will now be presented in this order.

How to Get to the Net

The player should go to the net only after preparing the way by means of a shot calculated to force a defensive return by the opponent. There are essentially four types of approach shots which can provide the opportunity for moving into the net position:

1. A forcing serve.
2. A forcing return of service.
3. A forcing shot made from any shallow return: that is, from a ball bouncing more than 9 to 10 feet from your base line.
4. An offensive lob.

Many of the techniques of making these forcing strokes are described in chapters 4, 5, and 7. Here they will be tied more specifically into the manner of getting in to net behind them.

On fast courts the present-day ranking tennis players always follow both first and second serves in to net. They have found by experience that rushing the net behind a powerful, deep serve will, in the majority of cases, set the stage for a winning point. From 10 to 23 percent of the time the serve elicits an error on the part of the receiver, as the latter is forced to attempt

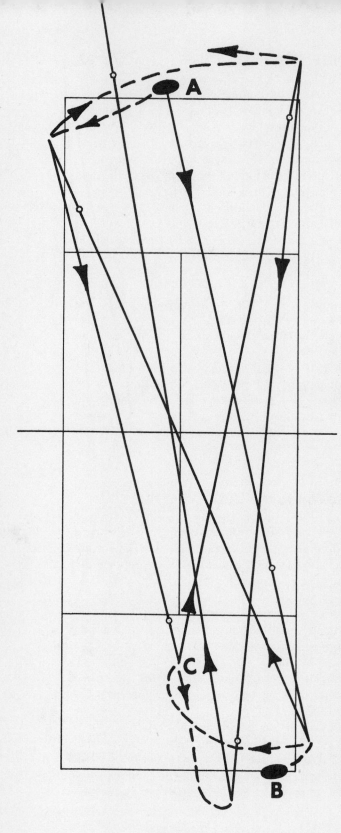

Figure 17

First Lesson in
the Value of Net Play

These diagrams illustrate the wrong and the right way to play a point often encountered by the weekend player.

Server A is your arch rival whose service you are desperately trying to break on a hot July morning. In the left-hand diagram you, receiver B, return the serve cross court and A returns a poor forehand to the middle. You seize the opportunity offered by running around the ball and hitting a fine forehand drive deep to the backhand corner. At your mercy, A runs puffing to make a desperation shot with weak backhand. But then you goof by just standing entranced, hoping for an error. Somehow your rival manages to lunge at the ball and hit back a slow backhand which floats 6 feet over the net and lands near the base line, which gives A plenty of

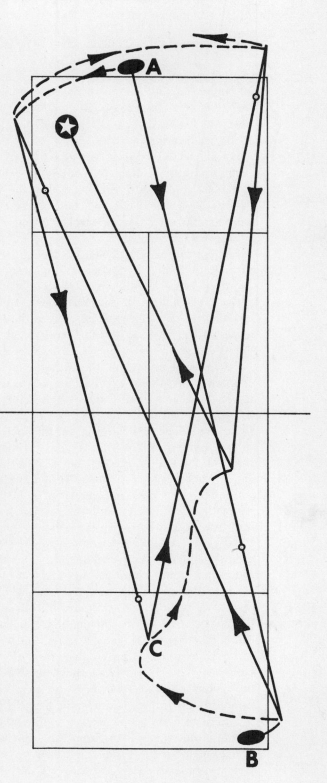

time to get back into position. All your hard-earned advantage was wiped out by one poor, feeble return, and you are forced to dash back to the base line to retrieve the ball. There, in trying too hard to recover the offense, you drive an off-balance forehand sailing over the base line to lose a point you once had in the palm of your hand.

The diagram on the right shows the same point as it should have ended. Having set the stage for the kill with the forcing shot to A's backhand, you should have capitalized on the situation by moving into the attacking position at the net. From this position, you have the whole forehand court open for an easy volley placement before your rival can reverse direction.

to play a low, delicate return out of reach of the volleyer. And, in about
50 percent of the cases, a successful return of service can be volleyed away
for a win on the first or later volleys. First volleys account for about 17
percent of all winners. Of the total points won, some 34 percent are won
at the net position.

On slow courts the serve, as we have already noted, is less potent. It
accounts for some 3 to 18 percent of points and provides a safe journey
to the net only 15 to 20 percent of the time, even among experts. First
volleys are far less effective and account for only 2 to 14 percent of the
winners. Subsequent net strokes bring the total number of winners at
net to some 25 percent.

For a serve to be sufficiently forcing to provide you with a good chance
to make a telling first volley, it must be hit deep. Against most players
the deep serve should be to the backhand side, as the return will ordinarily be weaker and, therefore, easier to volley. The only acceptable shallow serve is one so sharply angled to the forehand or backhand courts that
it causes the receiver to move considerably beyond the side line to reach
the ball.

To impress upon you the importance of this, remember, as stated in
chapter 4, that deep serves allow you to win two out of three points. Even
if you lack a powerful serve, it is wise to follow it to net on occasion
in order to rattle the receiver. When, on any given point, you do decide
to hit your deep serve and go in, the speed and direction of your approach
run are both vital. You have to get your foot over the base line as you hit the
serve and really sprint for the net. Getting halfway to net is murder—if
you cannot get way in so as to avoid difficult half volleys, you'd better
stay back. The best volleyers run in fast four or five steps and, as they
reach the area just behind the service line, bring the feet into the same
line and make a hop with the weight equally balanced on both feet. (This
is why you can see a worn area near the service line after a few matches on
a grass court.) While so doing they anticipate or see the direction of the
return and then continue their forward motion to intercept the ball as
close to the net as possible. Of course, in the case of a lob, they would
reverse direction and prepare to hit an overhead. The best path to
the net depends on the bounce point of the serve. The principle to remember is that you should run to the net nearly along the bisector of the angle
of possible returns, arriving at the volleying position with weight well
balanced. You should favor the down-the-line side of the bisector because
the faster return can be made on that side. This is explained simply by
means of diagrams as shown in figure 18. Note carefully how important
it is to be as close to the net as possible (6 to 9 feet) and positioned laterally
within a matter of inches from the point which gives you best court coverage. Remember that from most parts of the court the receiver has room to
pass you on either side. If you are a step out of position or if you arrive off

balance, the receiver is presented with a relatively simple passing shot.

There are other things which are helpful to keep in mind when going to net behind a serve. Most opponents have certain habits which, when diagnosed, will provide you with an advantage in getting to the proper volleying position. A review of figures 11 and 14 on returns of serve will assist by providing such helpful hints as:

a. Most deep serves are returned cross court. This is particularly true for serves to the backhand court, especially the forehand corner. The smart server should favor the cross-court side of his proper approach path just a bit if he finds an opponent follows this standard pattern for returns.

b. Shallow serves to the forehand court are usually returned down the line. This means the server should be prepared to protect this area while moving in to net.

c. Shallow serves to the backhand court are returned cross court in the majority of cases. The server must be aware of this in order to have a chance of successfully volleying such returns.

d. While the server is well-advised to play these percentages, it is important in doing so to note any giveaway motions by the receiver which will indicate either a cross-court or down-the-line return. The reason this is so important is that returns to either side are by far the most difficult for the net-rushing server to handle, as one must extend one's reach to the maximum in order to meet the ball thus returned.

In going to net behind other shots, such as return of service, ground strokes, or offensive lobs, many of the principles given for the serve apply. The approach shot must be hit deep, in the great majority of cases, in order to be effective. Deep forcing shots are easier to make from a weak, shallow shot, whether a serve, volley, or ground stroke. Also, it is much easier to get to the net if you start your run from a point already partway there. Some 90 percent of such journeys to the net begin by taking advantage of a weak, shallow shot landing more than 10 feet from your base line. To attempt to go in from deeper in the court is too risky. The forcing shot favored is deep to the backhand corner. This is not only because it is the weaker side, but also because a lob return usually permits a good chance at a forehand overhead, whereas a lob from the forehand corner may have to be hit with a difficult backhand overhead. There are, of course, exceptions. The professionals almost invariably hit the forcing shot down the line, because this maneuver provides the shortest path to the proper volleying position. They reserve the cross-court approach shot for cases when the opponent is out of position. Among lesser players the cross-court approach hit deep to the backhand is used much more often because

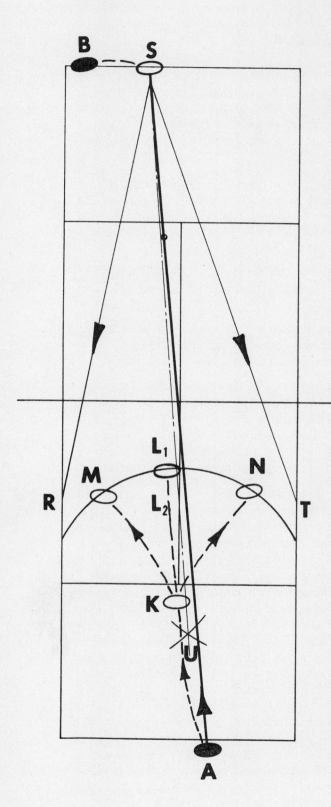

Figure 18

Going to Net Behind Serve

On the left is depicted the simplest case when the serve is to the middle. The possible angle of return is RST and the bisector of this angle is SU. The best path to the net is just a few inches on the down-the-line side of SU, since a slightly faster return can be hit down that side. The server, running in, pauses momentarily for a balanced hop at point K and then moves normally toward point L_1 or some other point such as M or N, depending on the direction of the return of service. Note that for every foot closer to the net along the L_2 to L_1 line, the server gains by having about 1 foot less width of court to cover. A driven return off a fast service seldom gives the server enough time to get in much closer than a step inside the service line. However, the server has a chance to cover such shots, because a hard drive cannot be hit at a wide angle along lines SR and ST, as it will sail over the side line.

On the right is shown the proper approach following a serve wide to the backhand corner. From point E, receiver B has a wider effective angle of return, DEF. The reason for this is, in large measure, the speed of the return. Whereas, just as in the case of the lefthand diagram, any angled return along line ED must be hit delicately, the long down-the-line shot to point F can be hit with blistering speed. This means that a server standing along the bisector G would have an easy time protecting the left side, but would be wide open for a fast passing shot down the line. To compensate for this and gain best command of the net, the server must approach the net on a line about 3 feet on the down-the-line side of the bisector to point L. Notice once again the advantage proximity to the net provides by decreasing the width of territory the volleyer must cover. The limit of the volleyer's forward advance is set by the ability of the opponent to lob effectively.

These diagrams also serve to illustrate the difference between the so-called center theory and the corner theory. On the left the advance to the net is from a ball hit to the center. This has the advantage of giving the opponent the smallest angle for a passing shot but has the disadvantage of allowing a return, often with the forehand, from a spot that is a perfect position to await your next volley. On the right the angle serve to the backhand gives the opponent a wider angle of return for a passing shot, but as volleyer you have offsetting advantages. Your approach shot forces the opponent to run and reach for the ball while trying to execute a passing shot from the weaker backhand side. And the court is open for a winning volley down the other side.

Knowing the correct position to take at the net against your opponent is an invaluable asset. Inches often make the difference between making your volley effectively or being passed or forced to err.

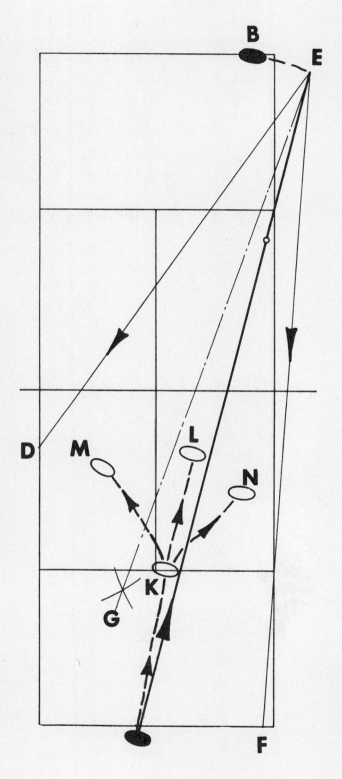

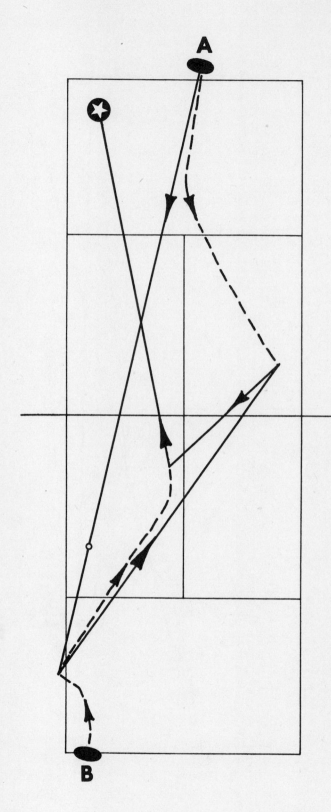

Figure 19

Going to Net Behind Return of Service

It is not often that a receiver gets an opportunity to go to net on a return of serve. Such openings occur only when the serve is shallow, as shown in this figure.

On the left is the classical approach against the net-rushing server. This is the exception to the rule that approach shots must be hit deep. Receiver B moves way in on a shallow second serve and plays a sharply angled cross-court dink to force the server to volley or half-volley up from close to the net. Knowing that just about the only shot server A can play is cross court over the low part of the net, receiver B moves in toward the middle

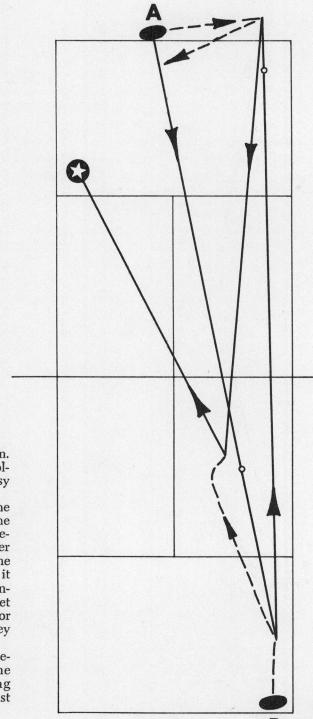

voleying position as shown. B's perfect tactics permit a volley of the return for an easy placement.

On the right is shown the proper approach shot when the server, A, does not come in behind a shallow serve. Receiver B moves rapidly to take the ball on the rise and plays it deep down the line. B continues moving forward to the net position and is rewarded for this action with an easy volley for the point.

These two patterns are repeated often, whenever the server is guilty of serving badly, whether the court is fast or slow.

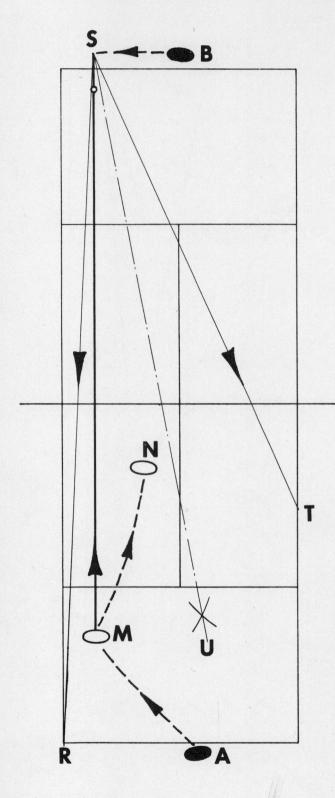

Figure 20

Going to Net Behind a Ground Stroke

These diagrams illustrate two methods of getting to the net after a shallow return to point M. On the left is the manner which the top players usually employ. They hit down the line deep and move in to the net to point N on the down-the-line side of the bisector SU of the possible angle of return RST. Note that the distance player A has to run to get to the proper net position is a minimum.

On the right is the method often used by weekend play-

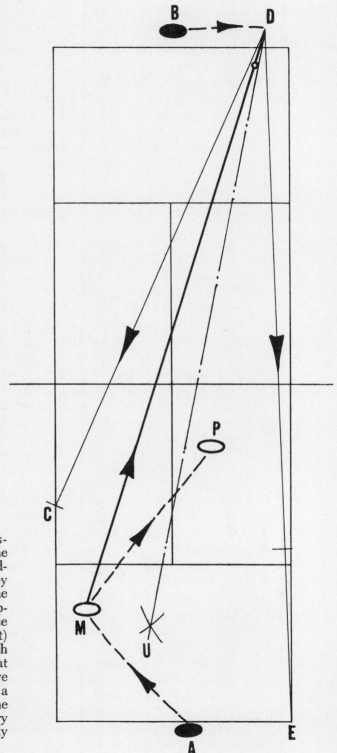

ers. They choose the cross-court return deep to the backhand in order to take advantage of the fact that they expect a poor return from the backhand side of most opponents. But note in this case how much farther (4 to 5 feet) player A has to run to reach the proper volley position at point P. An expert would have much more time to whip a passing shot down the line along DE, which is the very reason the top players usually avoid this tactic.

the return will usually be weaker from that side. Various methods of getting to the net are shown in figures 19 and 20.

The ground-stroke approach shots are among the most beautiful in tennis. No one who ever saw a Perry, Kramer, Laver, Ashe, or Connors go in to net behind a running forehand drive can forget the picture of balance, timing, rhythm, power, and speed. The whole operation of moving to the ball, stroking it, and running to the net appears to be one fluid, devastating motion.

Proper Volleying Positions and Anticipation

The proper volleying position at net is that point on the court which gives you the best chance of playing offensively your opponent's return. To volley offensively, it is best to be close to the net in order to hit down on the ball. But you cannot move in too close, lest you be lobbed. The best compromise is to stand 6 to 9 feet from the net, depending in part on your height and agility. This means that the proper volleying position for most cases is in the center of the court astride the line that divides the service courts at a point 6 to 9 feet from the net. We will refer to this as the basic volleying position.

But you must not assume that once you have reached the basic volleying position you can afford to remain glued to the spot. It is possible for an opponent to pass you from almost any point on the court, so your objective is to be sure you can get your racket solidly on the ball. This entails shifting your net position according to your opponent's position and type of stroke. Unless you can anticipate the direction and type of passing shot, you stand to lose the point.

Adjustment of net position to take into account the opponent's position has already been mentioned in the preceding section. A further description of the factors to consider is given in figure 21.

Anticipation is an art and, as with all arts, you have to spend time developing and sharpening your talents. To anticipate you must violate one of the cardinal rules of tennis—you have to take your eye off the ball.

There are four steps in anticipation. The first starts with your own shot. As a result of placing the ball in a particular spot and knowing your own position and that of your opponent, you should have a good idea what the return is likely to be.

The second step is to gather some intelligence data on the opponent. Most players have favorite shots, habits, or motions which give away the type of shot they are about to make. The style and method of stroke production employed often provide important hints. Time spent in studying your opponent in earlier matches will pay off handsomely. For example, a player with top spin is more likely to pass cross court than one who uses a flat drive. Often you will note that a player may fool a good opponent once by some trick shot, but the second time the same thing will backfire. This is because the good player has noted some giveaway motion, memorized it carefully, and used it to spot the same shot whenever it is next employed.

The third step is that of concentrating on the position and motions of the opponent as he or she prepares to strike the ball. In accomplishing this you have to take your eye off the ball and watch the overall actions of the opponent. This means noting the position of body, feet, arms, backswing, and racket. They telegraph the motion of the racket and the angle and speed with which it will contact the ball. This then permits you to predict the direction, speed, and spin of the shot so that you can move to the proper place and be prepared to make the return. While it may seem difficult to take all these signs into account in one quick glance, you will find it is actually fairly easy to learn with some practice and experience. For example, it soon becomes obvious that a ground stroke will be hit cross court if the ball is struck a bit in front of the player with a racket motion from the side lines toward the center of the court, and down the line if the ball is struck a bit late with a straight through motion (see figure 22).

The fourth and final step in anticipation is to learn how to take maximum advantage of your knowledge. Half the art of anticipation is hiding the fact that you have anticipated your opponent's shot until just the proper split second. If you move too soon to intercept the shot, your opponent will cross you up by changing direction, and if you wait too long, the ball will pass you. You must learn to time your move with great accuracy. Then, finally, you should shift your attention from the opponent to the ball and fix your eyes firmly upon it until you have executed your stroke and are ready to start the anticipation sequence once again. The first move is to get back into position—normally, the basic volleying position.

The ability of the experienced player to anticipate an opponent's intentions is truly remarkable. We attended a long match between Gonzales and Hoad once just to collect information on this point. To our amazement, only twice during the entire contest did these two great players get caught on the wrong foot! In other words, they were essentially always moving in the right direction to meet the ball and were never embarrassed by zigging when they should have zagged, as often happens among weekend players. To accomplish this feat certainly requires a superb sense of balance and a perfect grasp of the four essential steps in anticipation. A few selected points shown in figures 22 and 23 illustrate anticipation in action.

It behooves the player who is trying to improve to learn also how to counter the anticipatory powers of an opponent. The way to do this is to fake shots from time to time and to develop the habit of starting all your strokes with nearly the same motion. This will tend to confuse your opponent and to hide your intentions until it is too late.

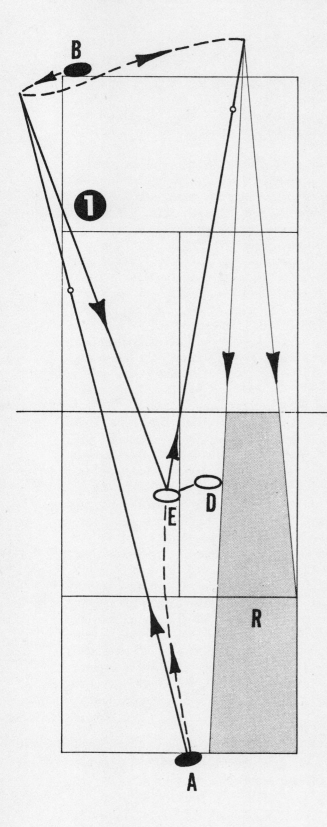

Figure 21

Lessons in Anticipation

The first step in anticipation is to know the situation. Here are two typical points where this knowledge is vital.

The lefthand diagram is a simple example of anticipation. Server A has run receiver B off the court a bit with a slice serve and then volleyed the return of service cross court to the open area. However, the volley lacked pace, and server A notes that the opponent can reach the ball after a long run. So A has to decide how best to cover the net. If you are server A, you should watch your opponent, B, not the ball. You will note that B is running diagonally away from the net and reaching with arm extended to play the ball slightly behind the body, while swinging down the line. With such a swing from this position B cannot hit cross court but will have to play down the line into the cross-hatched area (R) with a drive, low slice, or lob. Therefore, your next step is to move toward point D to be in proper position while continuing to diagnose which type of shot will be played. From point D you obviously have only a short distance to move to cover any type of return and play a forehand volley or overhead cross court to area 1 for the point. On the other hand, if you had remained near the center of the court at point E, a desperation drive down the line by receiver B might well have stolen what should have been an easy point.

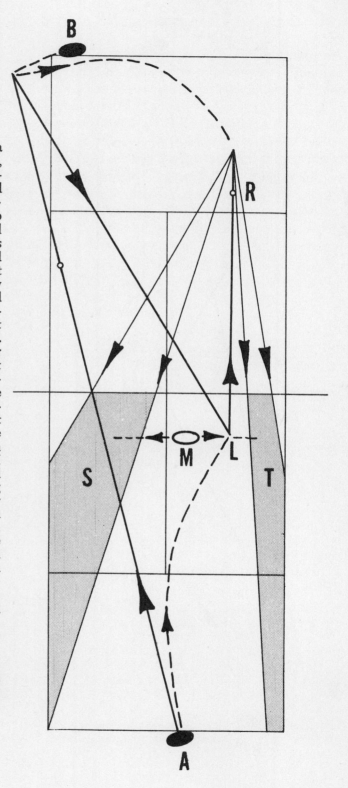

On the right is shown a tougher problem. As server A, you are forced to make a difficult first volley at point L and succeed only in making a shallow, low-bouncing volley to point R. This puts you in real trouble, and quick thinking is imperative. First you should decide that it is unlikely that receiver B will try to lob a low ball. This means you should stay close to the net to minimize the area you must protect against B's passing attempt. The whole left side of your court is open for a passing shot to area S. But if you start running too soon to cover the logical return to this area, receiver B will change the shot and chip one down the line to area T. The best solution is to move back to point M between the two areas and pause there a moment, being careful to maintain proper weight balance so that you can move in either direction. While poised, you must take your eye off the ball and study your opponent for a fleeting instant. Here is where knowledge of B's style is priceless. Having diagnosed the side down which the opponent appears committed to try to pass you, you then proceed to scramble for the shot with throttle wide open and eyes glued on the ball. Sometimes a brief prayer helps at this point.

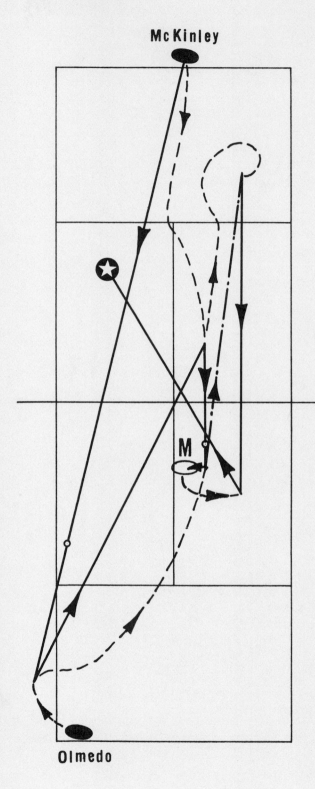

McKinley

Olmedo

Figure 22

Anticipation in Action

These two points were taken from a match between two fast players, Alex Olmedo and Chuck McKinley, during the 1959 U.S. National Championship at Forest Hills.

On the left server McKinley attempts a drop volley as his first volley. However, it is anticipated by Olmedo who plays a lob return. This shot McKinley anticipates in time to move back quickly and get set for an overhead and, presumably, an easy point. But "the Chief" is not to be denied. He moves quickly to his left to attract the attention of McKinley and pauses at M as he sees McKinley set himself a bit early for an overhead down the line. Then he sprints for the side lines and makes a miraculous cross-court volley from the overhead smash for the point as his opponent gasps in amazement.

On the right it is Olmedo's turn to be amazed. The point begins with Olmedo, the serv-

Olmedo

★

N

McKinley

er, playing a short volley. Mc-
Kinley tries to pass him cross
court, but Olmedo anticipates
and plays a drop volley. But
McKinley sees this coming
and lobs well over Olmedo to
the base line. This is retrieved
by Olmedo and returned with
a drive to the middle on
which McKinley tries to fool
him with a drop volley. However, "the Chief" sees this immediately and roars in to take
advantage of a perfect passing
opportunity. In this delicate
situation McKinley concen-
trates with every fiber to diagnose Olmedo's next move. By
good fortune he sees that Olmedo's feet and backswing
telegraph an angle shot to his
backhand. He decides to
pause just long enough at N
so that Olmedo cannot change
direction, and then dives to
his left. His resulting cross-
court volley for the point
brought forth well-deserved
cheers from the gallery.

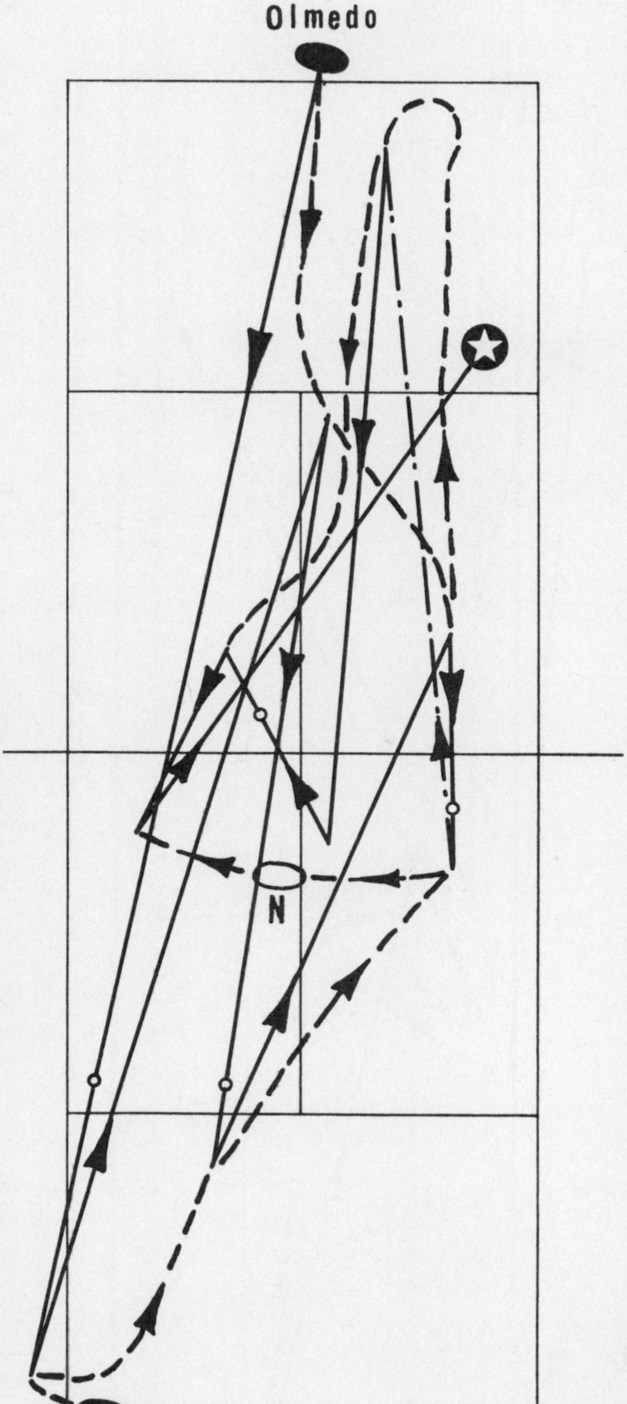

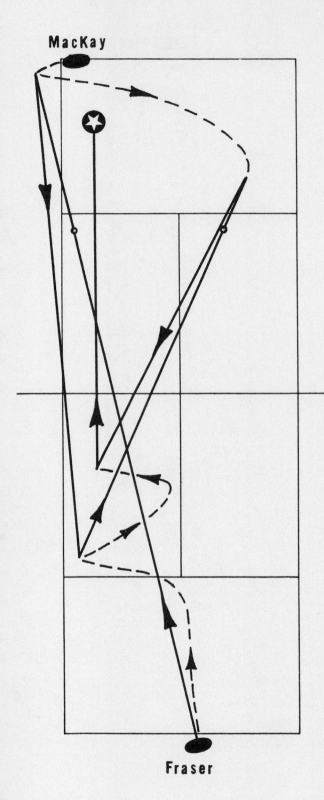

MacKay

Fraser

Figure 23

Great Anticipation

These are two points played by Neale Fraser in the 1959 Davis Cup Challenge Round which illustrate his great ability to anticipate.

On the left his serve is returned beautifully down the line so that he is barely able to half-volley rather feebly cross court, presenting Barry Mac-Kay with an easy passing opportunity. In this desperate situation Fraser starts back toward the middle of the net while keeping a careful eye on MacKay (not the ball), and slowing his momentum so that he can reverse direction if necessary. The split second he sees that MacKay is committed to try to pass by hitting cross court behind him, he reverses and lunges for the ball to pull off a great saving volley for the point.

On the right Fraser, as receiver B, returns the ball at MacKay's feet, forcing him to play a weak volley. Fraser tries to chip a passing shot down the line but MacKay anticipates this and moves over to volley. Again Fraser watches MacKay rather than the ball and notes that he is about to volley the ball in front of his body with his racket moving from side line toward the center — positive proof the shot will be cross court. So Fraser, now at point M, turns his attention back to the ball and to pouring on the speed. As a result, he is able to just reach the ball and to execute a fine volley down the line to win the point.

Proper Placing of Volleys and Overheads

Once you attain the net, the experts all agree, you have to go for the kill. If you cannot and are forced to play a defensive volley, by all means hit the ball deep. Just remembering and carrying out these two commandments will go a long way toward making your net play effective.

In championship tennis on fast courts, once the serve and return of serve are executed, three out of every four points are won at net. The importance of developing a decisive volley is, therefore, obvious. Just to poop the ball back gives the opponent an open invitation to pass you on the next shot. The better players, except in rare instances, hit uncompromisingly for the opening and the point.

The most important volley during a point is the first volley, since it sets the stage for the ultimate outcome of the point. In today's tennis the first volley is usually made off the return of service. The first volley is not only the most important, it is also the most difficult to make because of the long run required to reach the ball. This means that it is essential to have a clear understanding of the tactics which should be employed. Therefore, in order to evolve a sound basis for tactical instruction, hundreds of first volley points involving numerous top-flight players were recorded and studied. From this emerged a clear pattern which should be mastered by beginner and expert alike. A summary diagram showing the positions from which first volleys should be made and the areas into which they should be hit is given in figure 24. It is difficult to overemphasize the importance to the singles player of having this overall picture of first-volley tactics clearly stamped in his memory. Once this is accomplished, it is easy to proceed to the understanding of individual point situations.

When making the first or subsequent volleys, sound tactics, it must be remembered, also involve going for the kill. This generally means hitting the ball where the other fellow isn't. There are a number of types of openings for volley placements, such as:

1. A wide-open court, created by a great approach shot, which provides an opportunity where almost any kind of volley can win, even if stroked by your ailing grandmother.

2. A small opening into which you must volley with great speed in order to beat your opponent.

3. A small opening into which you must play a low-bouncing ball just out of reach of your opponent by executing a soft or spinning volley.

4. A surprise opening which you obtain by catching your opponent moving in one direction and punching your volley neatly to the rear. Often one false step is all you need for such openings.

5. A created opening which you accomplish by deliberately faking one type of volley and then changing direction or speed at the last mo-

ment in order to fool your opponent. This is particularly effective when one fakes the deep volley and hits a deft stop volley.

When in doubt, or when none of these five opportunities for a volley placement occurs, you should volley deep, usually to the backhand. But the most important thing is to keep the ball deep, as the opponent will have much less chance to pass you with the return. This is especially true if you are forced to reach wide and hit a defensive volley—here the deep volley gives you time to get back into position. Such volleys should be hit down the line, as flicked cross-court attempts will result in too many errors.

Some of the aspects of placing the volley are illustrated in figure 25.

Much the same thing can be said about the placing of ground strokes hit from inside the service line. You should go for the kill whenever possible. When in doubt, the best practice is to hit deep down the line.

The overhead is the most lethal stroke in tennis. The general rule is to hit all out for the kill whenever you are closer to the net than a point about 5 feet from behind the service line. From farther back the ball should be blocked back deep in order to keep the opponent pinned to the base line, and to give the striker time to get back in to the net position.

The overhead is usually placed deep in one corner or the other if hit from the neighborhood of the service line. From closer in, it is best to angle the overhead to open country for an almost certain point. It is important to remember two additional things. Overhead errors are 75 percent netted and only 25 percent outs. So hit them deep, hard, and accurately.

When selecting the spot to aim the overhead, it is necessary to glance at the opponent just before you stroke the ball in order to see which way he or she is committed to move. It is most embarrassing to forget this important detail. Every player cringes at the memory of a lost point already counted as won after smashing a tremendous overhead, only to look up and find the opponent there waiting with a diabolical grin and a perfect passing shot coming off the racket. A celebrated case of this sort happened once to unsettle the great Von Cramm at Forest Hills. Playing on the end court of three, he smashed a savage angled overhead against Bitsy Grant and looked up in horror to find Bitsy, the scrambler extraordinary, two courts down the stadium expanse with his racket on the ball! When Bitsy's return failed to win the point, he rolled the entire stadium audience in the aisles by taking off his cap, bowing low, and yelling across the length of the stadium, "Baron, you are just too good!"

One final bit of advice to the volleyer—don't goof. When presented with a setup, don't oblige by making a spectacular error. After working hard to force the opponent into hitting up a feeble sitter, it is disconcerting, to say the least, to knock it into the net or out. During the course of a three-set match the experts only goof two or three times. Take your time, watch the ball, don't overhit, and you should be able to reduce drastically the number of goofs.

Figure 24

A Composite Picture of Tactics for the First Volley When Serving to the Forehand Court

This diagram warrants careful study, as it contains a world of information on the first volley. Data taken from many matches provide the basis for valuable instruction on proper areas from which to make the first volley and where the volley should be placed. With this understanding of what happens on the average, it will be easy to develop the habit of making the proper move during individual points.

Your overall objective as server A, in making the first volley is to place the ball out of reach of the receiver, B, or to force B to play a defensive return. This means you must volley the ball outside the central Danger Area—when you do so you will win eight out of ten points. On the other hand, if you volley into the Danger Area, you give the receiver plenty of time to reach the ball and an excellent passing shot opportunity—in fact, you will win only four out of ten points.

The lower part of the figure shows first-volley positions. The most important thing to remember is that the server should get in as close to the net as possible by moving in to area D or C. (You should have time to reverse yourself if you anticipate lobs properly.) If you are slow and get caught in area A, you will be in serious trouble. First, you are likely to make an error or

be passed, particularly if the ball is near either side line. And even if you do make the volley you will lose six out of ten points, as you will hit many shots up weakly and place about one third of them in the Danger Area. Getting to area B offers little improvement. From here you will win only about half the volleys you make, as you are pulled way out of position and will again hit about one third into the Danger Area. However, if you get in far enough to cut off the return of service and volley from within area C, the odds turn heavily in your favor. You should win seven out of ten times and volley not over 30 percent into the Danger Area. From area D you are able to hit down at an angle, drop-volley, or hit deep at will, placing only one in five in the Danger Area and winning nine out of ten points. A little more than half the volleys should be made from area C and about 10 to 15 percent each from areas D and B. The remaining 25 percent from area A are forced upon you usually because you have delivered a shallow second serve or are slow in moving to net.

The upper part of the figure shows the proper aim points for first volleys. The necessity of avoiding the Danger Area has already been noted. The most important thing to learn

Receiver

as server is that if you will just keep your first volley deep (in the speckled area within 10 feet of the base line), you will rarely lose. From deep it is almost impossible for the receiver to pass an alert net player. On grass, the favorite tactic of the experts in serving to the forehand court is to serve wide to pull the receiver off the court and then volley deep to area R in the opposite corner. This maneuver keeps the ball out of reach of the opponent and wins nine out of ten times. Shots are aimed effectively at the drop or stop volley areas only when volleying from up forward in area C or D. Angle volleys are also most effective when made from well up in the court. Note that the safe area T for angle volleys is longer and wider on the backhand side when serving to the forehand court. The selection of just which volley to make depends on the relative positions and movements of the players. When in doubt as to the proper volley, it is best to volley deep, as this puts the receiver on the defensive and gives you time to move to the best position for your second volley.

The diagram for serves to the backhand court is just the same except that the angle volley area T and the deep volley area R are reversed.

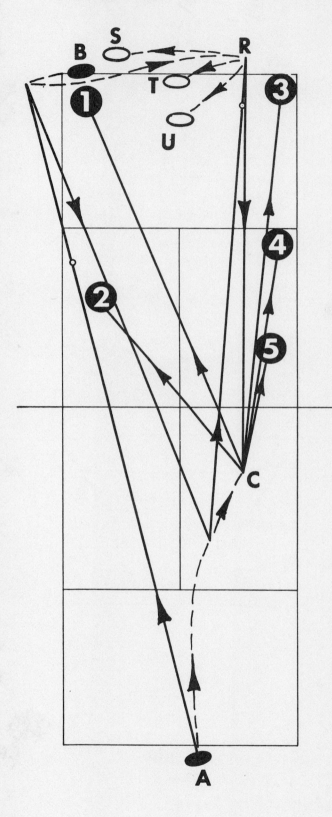

Figure 25

Placing the Volley

These diagrams illustrate some of the techniques necessary in going for the kill with the volley. The object is to hit the ball out of reach of the opponent. This means hitting to an open space or catching the opponent moving one way and then hitting behind.

On the left is shown a case where several choices are open to the volleyer; the purpose of the diagram is to point out the importance of making the proper choice. Receiver B has returned server A's first volley down the line, and server A is getting set to make a second volley from point C. In a brief moment server A must decide where to place the volley. Let us examine the problem as A notes the location and the direction and speed of movement of the opponent.

If receiver B hesitates too long at point R, it is best for the server to volley cross court to aim point 1 or 2. If hit from below the level of the net, the ball should be volleyed deep to area 1, and a high ball should be angled more sharply to area 2.

If receiver B hesitates at R and then runs hard toward point S, the volley should be hit behind, as B will be unable to reverse direction. A high ball can be hit severely to area 3; a ball hit from below the net can be sent spinning low to area 4 or drop-volleyed to area 5.

If receiver B moves to point T and is poised to move in any direction, server A must select the best shot based on the height of the ball. Often it is best to fake one way and volley another. When in doubt, the server should volley deep.

If receiver B suspects a short volley and moves in to point U, the volley should be hit deep behind to area 3.

On the right is shown what happens when each volley just misses in decisiveness against a determined defender.

The server, A, angles the first volley, but not enough to prevent the receiver, B, from reaching the ball and trying to chip a passing shot down the line. The server anticipates this and angle-volleys cross court to open country. But again it is not sufficiently sharp, and the receiver is able to reach the ball after a hard run. B tries to fool the server by a cross-court return, but the server again anticipates and hits a third volley angled slightly toward the side line for what seems to be an easy winner. But A has failed to put enough pace on the ball, and the receiver, after a desperate sprint, makes an amazing backhand passing shot down the line for a well-deserved win. This represents scrambling at its best.

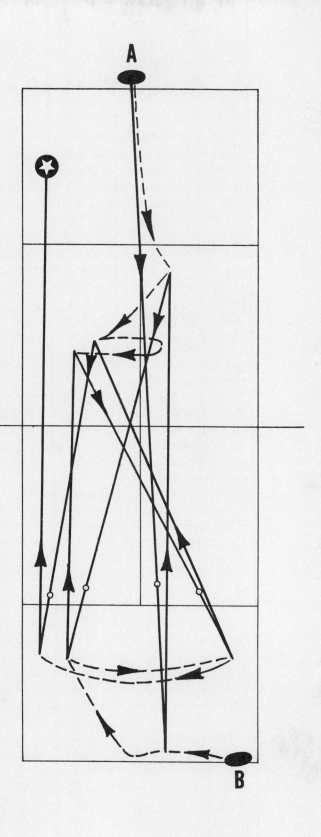

The Net Strokes

The volley is a short, crisp, punch stroke—like a boxer's jab—requiring little or no backswing and only a short follow-through. The only exception to this is the drive or swinging volley, a flat volley used to impart speed to a high soft return in order to put the ball away.

The net position is 6 to 9 feet from the net, depending on your height and speed of reflexes. The best net stance is a slight forward crouch with feet about two feet apart and weight on the balls of the feet for better agility. The racket is held with head slightly up, pointing at the net, so you can swing to either side with the same rapidity. The best grip is the continental, as the same grip can be used for forehand, backhand, and overhead.

The ball should be struck in front of you with wrist cocked slightly upward and firm. Your body should be turned sideways to the net when time permits you to step into the ball. If you must play a low volley, bend down to it—do not just drop your racket head. Bending the knees and getting down to the ball to maintain your wrist below the racket head is the secret of good volleying, as demonstrated by Billie Jean King in figure 26. You will stroke the ball more effectively partly because your eyes can follow the ball onto the racket with far greater accuracy when down near the level of the ball. The low volleys are defensive since you must hit up with little pace, whereas killers can be scored whenever the ball is above net level.

The volley stroke is made somewhat differently under certain circumstances. If you are forced to stretch to the limit to reach the ball, a flick of the wrist may be required to achieve speed and direction in the return. Low volleys which have to be played well in front of you are usually best played with a slicing motion. And if you wish to play a drop or stop volley, you must take the punch out of the shot with a loose wrist and little follow-through.

One way to picture the volley stroke is to consider that the racket and stiff wrist present a concave wall, much like a giant dish, from which the opponent's shot will rebound over the net. On low shots the wall is sloped upward, just as is the open racket face. At shoulder height the wall is perpendicular to the ground, just as the racket face is flat at the moment of impact. And above shoulder height the wall slopes inward and downward, indicating that the volley should also be struck downward with force.

The overhead is one of the most difficult shots in tennis to master, requiring absolute eye-on-the-ball discipline, as wind and sun can upset the shot. It is struck by most of the top players with the service (eastern backhand) grip or the continental grip. A major difference between the

a

Figure 26

Billie Jean King's
Standard Forehand Volley

b

Frame a. King is shown here in the classic anticipatory or ready position with knees bent, weight forward on the balls of the feet, racket in front with head high, cradled in the left hand, and set to volley from either side.

Frame b. Here she has pushed off on her left foot and started her shoulder and body turn as she watches and moves toward the approaching ball. Note the short preparation for the backswing with racket high.

c

d

Frame c. The reach for the ball is now at the point where the short back-swing for the volley is complete, with racket head above the wrist, the knees are bending to get down to the ball, and the left hand is extended for balance.

Frame d. This is the moment of truth as the racket meets the ball 6 to 10 inches in front of the body in perfect form to hit the ball down the line. (A cross-court volley would be hit a bit farther forward.) The knees are bent so that the racket head is above the wrist to give a firm hold on the racket and to allow the eyes to follow the ball right onto the strings. The firm wrist is laid back to direct the ball down the line. The racket head is tilted back to propel the ball up and over the net at the proper angle. The alert opponent should already be moving to the left to cover the return.

Frame e. Note here that the stiff laid-back wrist has followed through a short distance while the arm is extended forward only about 8 inches to complete the punching motion guiding the ball crisply, deep down the line. The right knee is so low it almost touches the ground.

Frame f. Finally, she has brought her racket forward in perfect balance and is rapidly regaining her ready position to await the opponent's return. Remember that no stroke is completed until you are back in position for the next shot.

overhead and the serve is the angle of the racket face at the moment of impact. The serve, you will recall, is hit with a stationary ball and the racket is drawn across the ball to impart a spin. Against a moving ball it is most difficult to avoid an error by any such tactics. Therefore, the overhead is properly played by turning the wrist so that the racket meets the ball with a flat face or with slight slice for control. Direction is imparted by wrist and arm motion, not spin.

The overhead is similar to the flat serve in almost all particulars: the ball is hit from the top of the service windup with body turned sideways to the net until the moment of impact. The ball is struck about a foot in front of the body, the only difference in stroke production being that the ball is ordinarily hit down a bit more and the feet may well be off the ground in the familiar scissors kick. If the lob is deep and accurate you may be forced to block the ball back deep, rather than hitting out at an overhead or letting the ball bounce and running back fast in order that an overhead stroke may be played.

Remember that anyone with an adequate serve can have an adequate overhead with a reasonable amount of practice. A major problem with the average player is that the overhead is generally one of the least practiced of all shots.

The backhand overhead is doubtless the shot most often avoided by all classes of players—everyone tries desperately to run around lobs to get them on the forehand side. The reason, of course, is that very few players can hit a backhand overhead with any pace. It is far safer to block such shots back deep or angle them off rather than to try to hit them hard.

The half volley is a shot to be avoided wherever possible, as it is strictly a defensive, difficult-to-control shot used to try to save a situation when you are caught out of position. Even the greatest of players are seldom able to hit this delicate shot consistently.

The proper method of stroking the half volley is to bend the knees to get down to the ball, take a short backswing with racket face open sufficiently to lift the ball over the net, and hit firmly through the ball with a short, controlled follow-through.

Figure 27

Billie Jean King's Overhead

Frame a. Here we catch King at the end of the preparatory hop as she *turns* and pushes off with her left foot to move back to get under the lob.

Frame b. As she starts to move back she immediately raises her racket, which is a necessary motion to get ready for the stroke.

Frame c. Note that as she turns and continues rapidly backward she watches the ball very intently. The problems of wind and sun make it absolutely essential to watch the ball right into the racket.

Frame d. At the start of the backswing she has her racket arm straight, knees bent, body sideways to the net, left arm out for balance, and eyes on the approaching ball.

Frame e. She is now in turned position under the ball as she continues her backswing, racket high and left arm extended. She is setting her weight on her right foot with knees bent ready to leap.

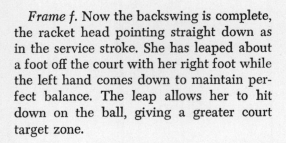

Frame f. Now the backswing is complete, the racket head pointing straight down as in the service stroke. She has leaped about a foot off the court with her right foot while the left hand comes down to maintain perfect balance. The leap allows her to hit down on the ball, giving a greater court target zone.

Frame g. At the moment of impact the racket arm is straight as in the serve, the right foot comes forward to put her weight into the shot while the left hand is tucked in and the body turns in the direction of the shot. From her position you can see she is aiming the smash at her opponent's backhand corner. The ball is hit almost flat; this not only is easier to do, but spin takes speed off of the shot. Her body is tilted back slightly to propel the ball deep in the court. The opponent better be on her bicycle by now to have a chance of returning this one.

Frame h. King has completed the scissor movement of the legs now as her right foot comes forward and her left foot comes down on the court. Note the beautiful wrist action as she brings the racket head down with great force in her follow-through. The footwork, balance, and grace are such that a dancer would be proud of this sequence of actions!

Frame i. The stroke is now completed with a long follow-through, and she is already turning to move rapidly back to the net and the ready position.

7

Base Line Play

In today's top-flight singles we are beginning to see a return to the long, exciting rallies characteristic of slow-court play so pleasing to the galleries. The abbreviated points exemplified by the big serve-and-volley game perfected by players like Gonzales on the fast court are being replaced by the play of the all-court prowess experts such as Tilden in the past and Connors and Evert in the present, who maneuver the opponent around the court with a mixture of blistering drives and spinning ground strokes until they force an opening for a killing placement. In addition to added excitement, the spectators also learn more from watching such all-court play, as their own abilities are closer allied to copying all-court strokes than the power strokes of the big game.

A clear and comprehensive description of the tactics of base line play is an extremely difficult undertaking. The reason for this is that style of play as well as players themselves vary so much in their effectiveness—those who do well against one type of play may do miserably against another. Only a master like Tilden can cope with any style by choosing to beat his opponent at his own game or by improvising to counter his strengths at every turn. The great tacticians, like Brookes, Lacoste, Riggs, and Laver, probed until they found weaknesses and then exploited them with precision, skill, deception, and determination. Others, like Vines, Helen Wills Moody, Maureen Connolly, Margaret Court, and Ashe at their peaks, merely blasted the opponent off the court with sheer power.

Because of the infinite variety of the base line game, it is practical to present only the key points in this chapter. These will involve sections on forcing shots, passing shots, defensive shots, and typical tactical mistakes. Following this will be the all-important section on methods of hitting the ground strokes. But before getting into these in some detail, there are a few overall tactics to master.

The most important thing to bear in mind is that base line rallies are essentially fencing operations. You must try to "move the opponent around" by one means or another in order to extract an error or a weak return. Moving opponents around may mean running them from side to side, mixing them up by changing direction, depth, speed or spin, or catching them going in one direction and hitting in the other. Whatever the method, once your opponent hits a bad shot which lands shallow (closer to the net than 10 feet from the base line), you should go for the kill by hitting a forcing shot and moving in to the net. While this is easier to do on a fast court than on a slow one, you must, nevertheless, take advantage of these all-too-rare opportunities whenever the opening is presented. Otherwise the opponent will recover position and you will have wasted the advantage you worked so hard to gain. For overpowering testimony to the importance of taking advantage of the short ball, remember that data from numerous matches show that seven of eight winners in base line play come as a result of capitalizing on a short ball.

The second thing to remember is to hit within your capabilities. To make errors, however spectacular, leads to naught, but to keep the ball under control and in play leads to victory over many an opponent.

Next, what should now be a familiar requirement, is to work at anticipating each move by your opponent in order that you may cover the wide expanse of court and move into position to make the return. Proper balance and position make this relatively easy, but a move in the wrong direction spells disaster. Between strokes you should ordinarily attempt to return to the basic base line position, which is at the center of the court about a foot behind the base line. In doing so you cannot afford to be leisurely. Concentrate particularly on anticipating the direction and length of your opponent's forehand as it is usually his or her best stroke. Remember that all those "effortless" players who are always in position really get that way by being tops at anticipation.

And, finally, in striving to improve your base line play, practice keeping the ball deep. This is the trademark of the accomplished player. Your opponent can seldom make a truly offensive return from deep court.

Forcing Shots

To become a good singles player you have to develop the ability to hit forcing ground strokes. These are the weapons with which defenses are pierced and openings are gained. As with all strokes in tennis, there are several varieties of forcing shots:

1. *Sheer power type.* Some players just hit the ball so hard to the corners of the base line that they either run their opponent into the ground, draw weak returns which can be put away, or force errors. Examples of typical points by the power players are shown in figures 28 and 29.

2. *Tactical type.* Most players are not equipped with overwhelming power, so they have to resort in part to cunning. This means being able to outthink or outmaneuver your opponent. Usually this entails a deceptive change of pace, spin or direction. Wise tacticians keep forcing shots low to prevent the opponent from lobbing effectively. In fact, on a wet court the smart player takes advantage of the low-bounce conditions and goes to net more often. As in the case of the volley, most forcing shots are hit to the backhand side because the return is usually weaker and lobs can generally be hit on your fore-hand side. Some typical points are shown in figures 30 and 31.

   Another trick of the tactician is to find a particular weakness of an opponent and then exploit it wisely. This means to exploit it only to gain certain crucial points, as overdoing it may cause your opponent to correct the defect. Since it is not possible to predict all the types of flaws you will encounter in various opponents over the years, we will have to be content here with just trying to emphasize the importance of discovering whatever weakness does exist. Perhaps an example of an actual case involving Davis Cup players will serve this purpose.

   We remember vividly a conversation we had one afternoon with a top player as we walked together from the dressing room to the stadium where he had an important match. He confided he thought he had detected a chink in the armor of his opponent (name omitted out of kindness). From watching previous matches he believed that his adversary had a tendency toward errors when forced to run wide and play a ball hit low and deep to his backhand. As our friend took the court we grabbed a seat near the base line and waited anxiously to see what would happen. Any anxiety was short-lived. On the very first point our friend hit a drive deep to his opponent's forehand and then sliced a ball low and deep to the backhand. His opponent, running at top speed, golfed the spinning ball into the bottom of the net. Seeing this, our friend walked quickly back to the spot where we were sitting and whispered with a broad grin, "The match is over." And it was—in three straight sets.

   In weekend play, weaknesses are more prevalent so that tactical

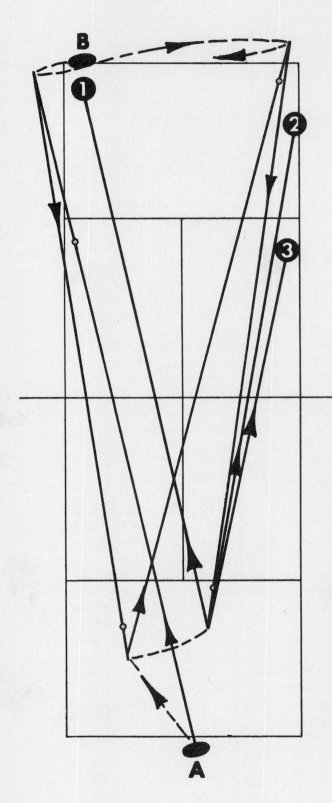

Figure 28

Classical
Forcing Shots

These diagrams show the murderous types of forcing shots which should be familiar to all who have watched tournament play.

On the left is a sequence which is so deadly the server can often win the point in any of three ways without even bothering to take the net. The server, A, has run the receiver, B, off the court with a serve to the forehand corner and then hit the return deep to the backhand to run B off the court on the other side. When this draws a shallow return, server A has three possible choices for a win. If receiver B is slow in moving back into position, A can drive the ball beyond B's reach to aim point 1. If, on the other hand, receiver B expects this cross-

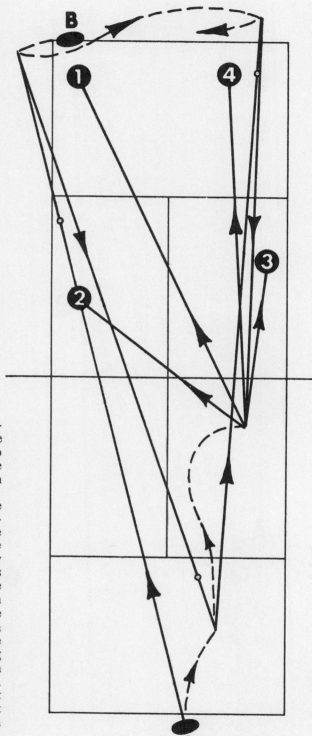

court return and starts running hard to the right, the server can hit behind B deep to aim point 2, or slice one shallow and wide to aim point 3.

On the right is shown the proper method of forcing following a weak return to the middle. The idea is to waste no time once an opportunity is presented. Server A drives deep down the line to the backhand, goes in to net on a line to guard against the expected down-the-line return and finds the court is wide open for a choice of winning volleys. Depending on when and where B starts to move, A can volley deep to aim point 1, angle volley to aim point 2, or volley behind B to aim points 3 or 4.

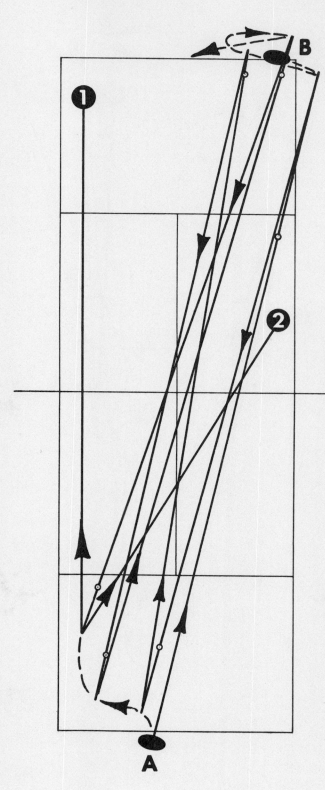

Figure 29

Taking Advantage of the Shallow Return

Much of forcing base line play is fencing for a shallow return and capitalizing on it.

On the left is shown a classic sequence often used by the great clay court players. The serve is kept to the backhand corner and a series of backhand exchanges is started. The purpose of the server, A, is to push receiver B farther and farther left until A draws a shallow return. Once this happens A can then crack one down the line to aim point 1. As the players put it, the receiver would need a bicycle to reach this one. If, in fact, B were pedaling fast enough to try to cover the down-the-line shot, the server can still earn a placement, by faking the drive and then changing direction and hitting a soft, sharply angled shot cross court to aim point 2 to wrong-foot the receiver.

On the right is shown another classic maneuver after a very shallow return. In this case the server has proceeded to run the receiver hard with a sequence consisting of a wide serve to the backhand, a slice wide and low to the forehand, and a drive deep to the backhand corner. Receiver B has just managed to get the latter back with a weak shot landing in the middle of the service court. Server A approaches the ball, fakes a hard drive to either corner to keep B deep, and then hits a delicate drop shot to aim point 1 or 2. In baseball parlance, the pitchers call this pulling the string. Such tactics are especially good if the court is slow or the opponent is slow or tired. Women use this shot against one another with telling effectiveness.

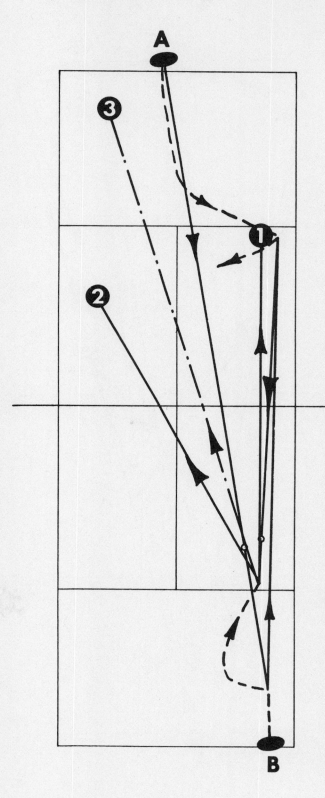

Figure 30

Classical Passing Shots

The success of the passer depends on forcing the net player to volley short—within a few feet of the service line at the maximum. Once you do this, you have to make your passing shot count by placing it carefully, but not trying to raise chalk dust with each shot. In fact, you win more points by drawing an error by making the volleyer reach than you do by executing a clean pass. On very short balls it is often best to hit the passing shot right at the chest of the volleyer to draw an error.

On the left is shown a favorite tactic for receivers against net-rushing servers. The serve is somewhat shallow, so receiver B moves in and hits the return early and low down the line. This catches server A near the service line, and A must reach far to the left to make the volley from near the ground. Receiver B should anticipate a volley hit up weakly and in a down-the-line direction. There is practically nothing else the server can do. Thus, receiver B should move in a bit and get set to capitalize on the short volley, as shown. B must watch the server as well as the ball. If the server starts to move to the center, the passing shot can be chipped safely

down the line to aim point 1.
And if the server is slow to
recover, the receiver has a
wide-open court to hit a
slightly topped passing shot
cross court—with room to
spare—to aim point 2. If the
server moves in close to the
net to try to cut off either return, an offensive lob can be
dumped neatly overhead to
aim point 3.

On the right is depicted one
of the most common passing
situations encountered against
the net-rushing server. Here
the return of service is a
sharply angled, low, cross-
court slice or dink which
forces server A to volley up.
A will usually do so cross
court, because the net is too
high to hit effectively down
the line. Sensing this, you can
get set for the passing shot.
This is a thrilling situation, as
it necessitates outguessing the
net player. A knows you will
go cross court to aim point 1
if he or she runs too far right,
or down the line to aim point
2 if he or she lingers. Against
a good net player you have to
note his or her actions and
hide your intentions to the
last second. If you do, you
have an easy winner, and, if
not, your opponent has an
easy volley for the point. So
be careful!

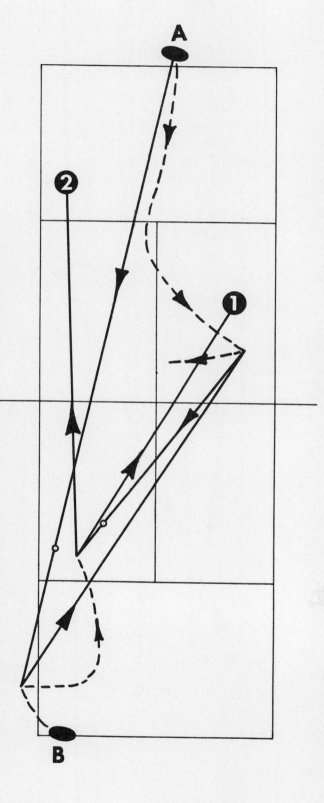

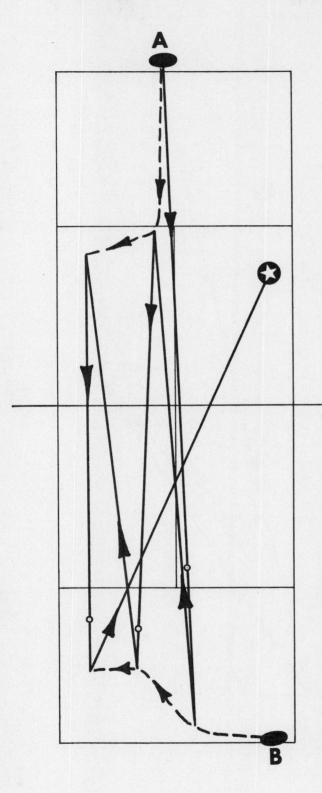

Figure 31

Engineering the Pass

While outright passing shots which whiz through narrow paths past the net player are beautiful to behold, it is much more likely that success is achieved only after two or more carefully selected shots, the last of which wins or draws an error. This figure shows two examples.

On the left, receiver B returns service cross court to a point near the service line. At this moment receiver B should sense the passing possibilities. Since server A is volleying from near the service line, A will probably not be able to play a truly forcing shot. So receiver B properly moves a step inside the base line, hoping for a short return. When server A obliges, B is ready to move in while observing the moves of the net player. As server A starts to cover the middle, B elects to chip low down the line. By this maneuver B forces server A to reach far for the ball and volley up. Since this should result in a weak volley down the line, receiver B gets set for such a return. When this happens, B has successfully created the needed opening. With server A way on the righthand side of the court, B can hit a cross-court passing shot for a well-deserved win. Or, if server A moves too rapidly cross court, receiver B can hit the passing shot behind A down the line.

On the right is shown a point played against Rosewall, with his opponent, A, engineering a fine passing sequence under the pro three-bounce rule. A serves to Rosewall's backhand, and the point begins with a familiar base line pattern of cross-court returns answered by down-the-line returns. Rosewall decides to take the net on his backhand down the line, and his opponent returns with a soft, low forehand to the middle to try to draw a short volley. He then starts moving a bit forward in expectation, so that it is easy for him to get set for the short return when it occurs. As he sees Rosewall move toward the middle, he decides to hit a delicate spinning, cross-court backhand dink just over the net. He properly anticipates that this will force Rosewall to volley up, so once again he moves forward to take advantage of the opportunity. He is rewarded for his excellent tactics by a weak volley which he, in turn, is able to volley away down the line to complete a beautiful exhibition of a passing sequence.

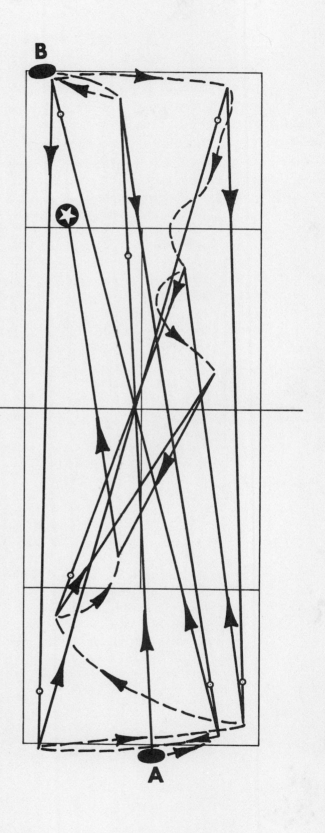

choices can often be broader. If your opponent likes to slug, deliver soft shots and spin. (If you hate spin, go to net.) If your opponent likes to come to net and you have trouble passing, get to the net position first. If your opponent hates to volley, draw him or her forward. If your opponent cannot run, use the drop shot.

3. *Continuous pressure type.* In a sense, the important business of just getting each ball back as deep as possible is a form of forcing game. This tactic often goads an exasperated opponent into becoming more and more impatient, and then he or she will start to make errors by overhitting the ball or trying shots which are too difficult to make with any consistency. Many a big hitter has been beaten by blowing up under this sort of subtle pressure.

Once the forcing game has created for you the opening represented by a short ball, move in and go for the placement. A good deep or angled drive or slice, or a drop shot from in close, should win most points, and a volley of any return will take care of the rest.

Passing Shots

To capture a set in tennis you have to be able to break the opponent's service at least once. This means it is an absolute must to have in your arsenal of weapons some effective passing shots if you are to win against the serve-and-volley demons of today.

Your chances of passing anyone at net depend in large measure on how far you are from the net at the moment you strike the ball. On balls which land within about 10 feet of the base line, your chances of passing a good volleyer are almost nil. But on any ball landing closer in, the odds should shift in your favor. Data taken from many matches serve to emphasize these statements. Successful passing shots are made only one in four tries (omitting errors) from a ball landing within 10 feet of the base line. However, from 10 to 18 feet (the service line) from the base line, two out of three passing shots are winners. And from within the service line, the volleyer is a sitting duck—the passer can beat him seven out of eight times. Before you think this is too easy, just remember you have to be able to anticipate and move in to reach the short volley in time before it can be turned into a passing shot.

Since the passer is presented with a short ball only about one in three times, you cannot afford to miss very often. An important part of not missing is anticipating when to expect a short ball and where it will probably land, so that you can get set for your passing shot. There are several typical opportunities on which you can capitalize, such as:

1. A return of service which forces the net-rushing server to volley up from the feet near the center of the service line is likely to result in a weak return, usually near the center.

2. Any return which forces the volleyer to reach far to one side will usually result in a short volley hit down the line.

3. Any return which the net player must half-volley will ordinarily be lifted with little pace. If you can anticipate the direction, you should have plenty of time to move to the right spot and note the best passing possibilities.

4. Any dink return which the net player must volley up from close to the net will usually result in a short volley hit cross court over the center of the net, since this is the lowest portion of the net.

In connection with passing, do not underestimate the value of the lob. It is not just a desperation shot to be used only when run off the court. On short balls the offensive lob is a powerful tool, especially when the shot is hidden (see figure 32). Masters of the lob like Laver, Connors, and Orantes often beat top opponents by using the well-masked lob in preference to other passing shots. And if the opponent is crowding the net or moving in, even a defensive lob is apt to become a winner. The professionals employ the lob extensively and expertly to keep the opponent from playing on top of the net. On a low-bounding ball, deep in the court, it is best to use the very high defensive lob. Both young and old tennis players can improve their game greatly by studying the use of the lob as demonstrated by these experts. They have perfected the offensive and defensive use of this important weapon and never hesitate to use it. The lob is the most underrated shot in tennis; all players would do well to practice it.

A number of base line and all-court plays to illustrate the infinite variety of tennis and the importance of a courageous defense are shown in figures 32 and 33.

Some typical tactical mistakes are illustrated in figures 34 and 35.

To extricate yourself from the defensive position represented by the base line area takes a combination of patience, skill, and determination seasoned with a proper amount of dash, daring, and imagination.

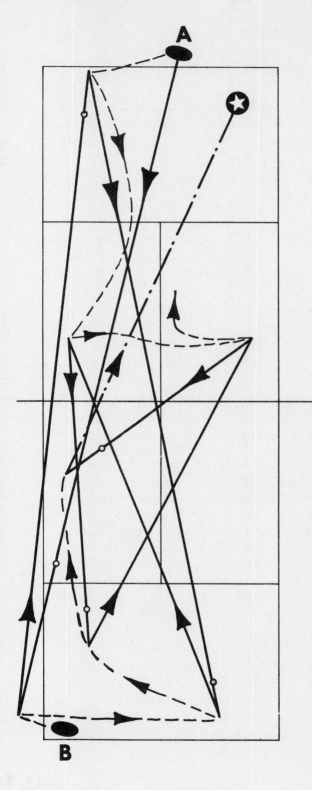

Figure 32

Defense and Scrambling

Here are two points which show the defensive touch of the pros. When in trouble, they set an example for all tennis players in their efforts to extricate themselves.

On the left Rosewall, the receiver, returns serve down the line and is promptly run wide to the forehand as his opponent takes the net. Here Rosewall hits a soft, topped forehand cross court which the opponent has to hit up a bit. This gives Rosewall time to cover the volley. From this point he hits a soft cross-court backhand dink which again forces the net player to volley up. At this moment Rosewall anticipates a cross-court return and moves forward. As a result, he is able to fake down the line and then lob the return beautifully cross court to the corner for a fine point.

Rosewall often crosses his opponent by hitting the unusual shot—a backhand lob down the line.

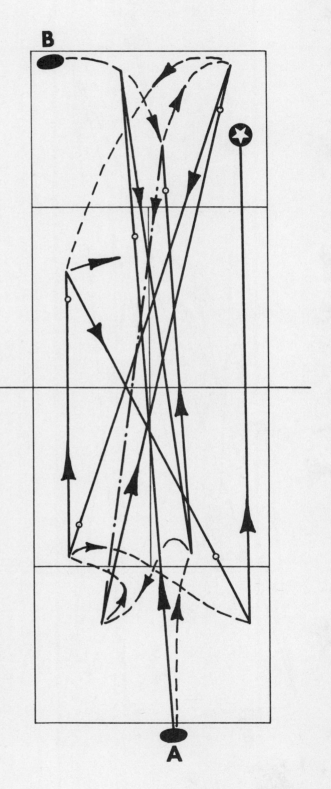

On the right Roy Emerson, server A, gets into trouble by making a short first volley. The receiver lobs and Emerson is just able to get back to block a backhand overhead deep to the corner. The opponent tries to catch him by hitting a cross-court passing shot as Emerson is going back in to the net. But Emerson anticipates in time to reverse direction and tries to cross up the opponent by dumping a little drop shot down the line. This is noted by the opponent, and he roars in to cover the shot. As he does so, Emerson is in a desperate position—he must anticipate the direction of the next shot. As he moves to the center, he sees the opponent reach around the ball toward the right side line which signifies a cross-court shot. At this, Emerson pours on the coal toward the side line and is just able to reach the ball and poke it down the line for a great win.

Figure 33

Never Give Up the Ship

In the tense moments of an important match, the players are keyed up to the point where they will pull off remarkable shots. This means two things: never assume the opponent will miss and never give up trying to retrieve the ball.

On the left is a fabulous point recorded in Davis Cup play. Server A serves wide to the backhand and volleys the return cross court for what would often be a placement. But the receiver is so fast in covering court that he is able to run past the ball and make a topped cross-court return. The server replies by dumping a little drop volley just over the net. Again the agile receiver gets to what might have been another winner and is able to lob deep. The server scrambles back, returns a deep lob, and rushes in to the net. The receiver tries to surprise him by hitting back another lob. As he sees the server will, indeed, have to play an off-balance overhead aimed to the backhand side, receiver B elects to take a gamble. He moves forward to cut off the shot and is rewarded by being able to block a volley down the line for a sensational win of a point seemingly lost at least twice!

On the right is shown a point played in a National Clay Court Championship. Here server A plays a deep cross-court forcing shot off the return of service and takes the net. Receiver B plays a delicate cross-court dink which forces the server to volley up short cross court. The tide now turns in favor of the receiver as he anticipates well and moves in to hit down the line. But the shot is not quite deep enough, and server A is able to reach the ball after a hard run. He plays a high defensive lob which receiver B gets set to put away in routine fashion. But his play is too routine. He fails to hide his direction so that the scrambling server is able to cover the ball and hit a sensational down-the-line passing shot for a win. And no one is more surprised than receiver B, who wrongly assumed the point was over and just stood there watching as though in a trance.

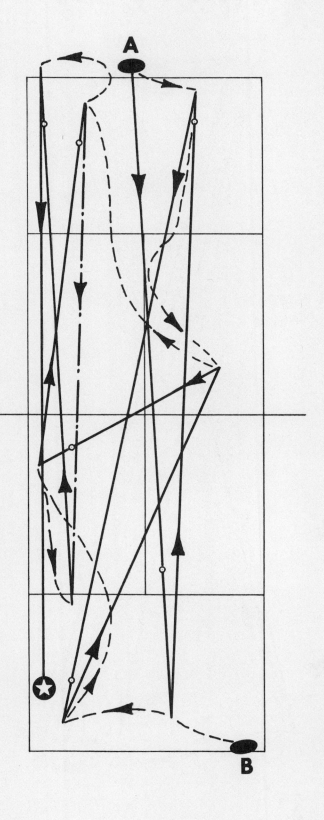

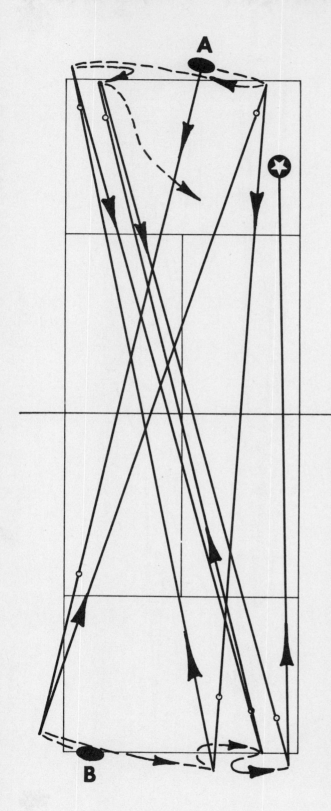

Figure 34

Tactical Errors

Even the top players make tactical errors at times. Perhaps it will be refreshing as well as helpful to the weekend player to show a few horrible examples.

The goof on the left was made by one of the top pros—we will, mercifully, omit his name. Here, after the return of service, an exchange of cross-court forehand drives is begun. After the third one, server A decides to take the net on still another cross-court forehand. In so doing he violates three principles—this makes his path to the proper volleying position the longest possible, gives the opponent the widest passing angle, and puts the ball on the opponent's strong forehand side. As a result, receiver B is able to drive down the line for an easy outright placement which almost any

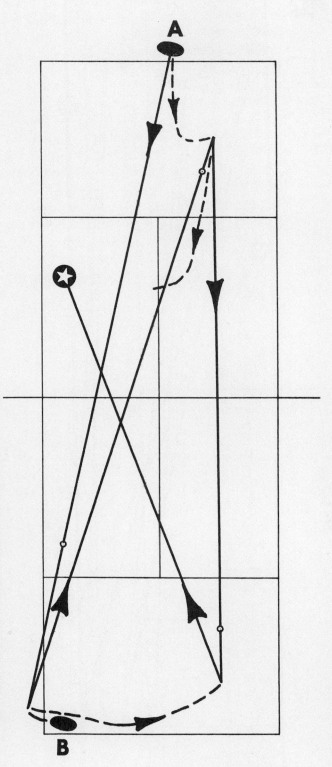

weekend player could also have produced.

The bad move on the right is typical in many a match. Receiver B has returned service a bit shallow cross court. So server A smells an easy win and decides to gallop in behind a down-the-line approach shot. But the forcing shot is not forcing at all. Despite the fact that it is too shallow and too near the middle, server A has a set mind and continues the move toward the net. This presents receiver B with a ridiculously easy passing situation. With server A caught back near the service line, it is simple to hit a cross-court shot to the wide-open spaces. Perhaps it should be noted that there is no law against changing your mind about going to net if you hit a poor approach shot.

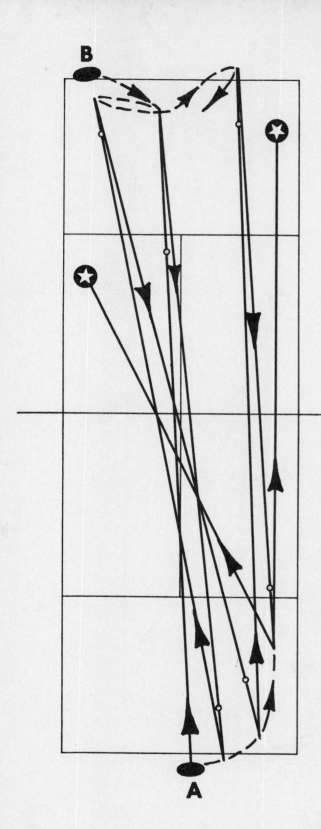

Figure 35

More Tactical Slips

Let us continue the lessons on what not to do.

On the left the point starts out well for receiver B, who makes a good, deep return of service and exchanges deep forehand drives. Next, server A drives fairly deep down the line. At this juncture receiver B hits just about the worst possible return—shallow back down the line. As will be seen from the diagram, server A has been handed the point on a silver platter. All that is needed is to hit a topped cross-court shot for a winner or wrong-foot the receiver by hitting back down the line.

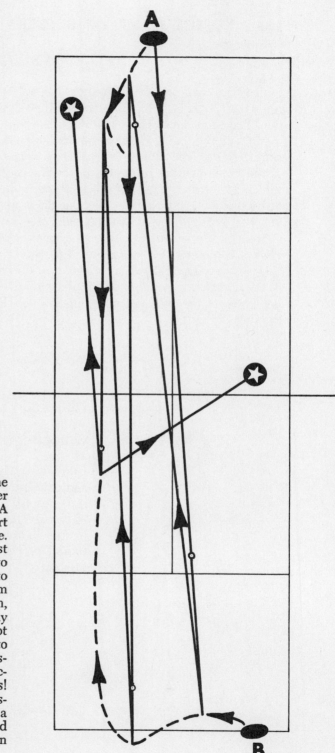

On the right is depicted the misuse of the drop shot. After a semideep return, server A tries a drop shot from a short distance inside the base line. Unless the opponent has just broken a leg skiing or gone to sleep, half the day remains to cover any drop shot hit from deep in the court. As shown, receiver B has merely to play a sharp cross-court drop shot or a drive down the line to win after such a tactical mistake. Yet this point was actually played at Forest Hills! Incidentally, this also illustrates how easy it is to win a point when playing a ground stroke at net as recorded in Table VI (see chapter 3).

The Ground Strokes

The forehand and backhand—the so-called ground strokes of tennis—are useful in direct proportion to their pace, depth, accuracy, and deception. Pace and depth come only from the perfect blending of those magic ingredients of any good athletic stroke—coordination and timing; or, in simpler terms, the ability to lean your weight and strength into the shot at the exact moment you strike the ball. Accuracy and the ability to place the ball you will learn by subtle shifts in ball-racket angles and in the distribution of your weight. The weight is about evenly divided between the two feet on shots down the right side line; on cross-court shots it is shifted to the left foot somewhat sooner. Deception is accomplished by always beginning the stroke the same way and setting the direction and spin or lack of spin at the last moment in the execution of the shot.

Two important pointers on ground strokes: bend the knees so that you get down to the ball and never neglect the follow-through—always finish the shot.

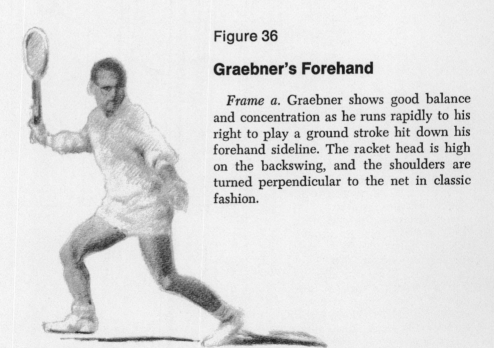

Figure 36

Graebner's Forehand

Frame a. Graebner shows good balance and concentration as he runs rapidly to his right to play a ground stroke hit down his forehand sideline. The racket head is high on the backswing, and the shoulders are turned perpendicular to the net in classic fashion.

a

Forehand Drive

The workhorse of tennis is the forehand drive, the staple of the game for most players. It can be the big stick with which to beat down your opponent or the last bulwark of defense when all else fails.

For purposes of initial illustration of the typical topped forehand drive we have selected a stroke sequence exhibited by Clark Graebner in figure 36.

b

Frame b. Here Graebner has reached the ball and planted his right foot to halt his run and prepare to stroke the ball. The racket head has dropped and will go below the ball in the familiar figure eight. The left hand is extended for balance.

Frame c. Graebner is just about to bring his racket up and over the ball to apply top spin. By his position you can tell he will hit the ball well in front of his left foot and direct the shot cross court. The shoulders are turning to impart force to the stroke.

Frame d. This figure shows clearly the application of top spin to the ball. The racket comes up sharply over the ball with a closed face. The forearm, wrist, and racket are in one straight line. The momentum of Graebner's run for the ball continues to carry his left foot over and forward for balance. Note how well bent the knees are kept to permit him to get down to the ball to watch it all the way into the center of the racket and to maintain balance.

Frame e. The stroke is perfectly completed with racket face closed and high over the left shoulder for complete follow-through. The left foot is now planted, and Graebner is about to start moving rapidly to his left to get back into the ready position at the center of the base line.

Backhand Drive

The backhand drive is executed on the same mechanical principle as the forehand drive. Properly hit, it can be just as effective as the forehand. The average player finds the backhand shot more difficult than the forehand, but actually it should be easier because you're swinging away from your body. Contrary to general belief, it should be an attacking and not a defensive weapon.

Figure 37

Baseball swing is the analogy used by Budge to describe backhand motion. He has likened it to the swing of Ted Williams.

The left arm is unusually important to a good backhand. To start with, it does most of the work in taking the racket back to the start-forward position. From this point it serves an equally vital function in helping achieve and maintain balance. An interesting and sound formula to follow is that of executing a perfect circle in preparing for and completing the shot. Wait for the shot from the squared position (always on your toes), pivot, swing, follow-through, and return to the original position, waiting for the next shot.

The backhand must be a fluid and continuous motion, not a series of separate acts performed one after the other. Properly executed, the steps are simple and related, creating a natural sequence without hesitation or acceleration. Starting with the anticipatory position in the backcourt, the right hand is relaxed on the handle, the throat of the racket cradled lightly in the left. As the ball approaches, you move into position, following the flight of the ball. That is of the utmost importance. The left hand guides the racket until the downward arc begins, when the right hand tightens its grip. At point of contact—approximately 12 inches in front of the right foot—the ball should be met waist high. If the bounce is low the knees should be bent more to meet the ball at its height. The shot should be made with a firm grip, the wrist straightening and locking naturally at the time of contact.

Next to that of Don Budge, perhaps the greatest backhand in modern tennis belongs to Ken Rosewall, the diminutive Australian. One of the most interesting points is that he hits the ball quite differently from Budge, using an underspin rather than a slight top-spin shot, which proves that there is more than one way to produce an outstanding tennis stroke. Players must adapt their own physical characteristics and natural feel for the game to the development of their stroke techniques. But the methods of all the great players have many points of basic similarity. Rosewall believes proper footwork is vital to a successful backhand. (To reach greatness, Tilden took off a whole winter to work on his backhand footwork and stroke.) The object is to get the ball just the right distance from the body for an uncramped, balanced swing.

Lobs

The forehand lob starts with the motions of the forehand drive, and then the action changes at the last moment to an upward motion with a shorter than normal follow-through. The offensive lob should be a surprise shot, so that it is vital to hide your intentions by employing your usual backswing. The best lobbers also roll the wrist a bit to put a top on the low, offensive lob in order to make the ball drop faster and bound away from the retriever.

a

Figure 38

Ken Rosewall's Backhand

Frame a. Rosewall has his weight a bit on his rear foot and his shoulders turned way back, elbow bent, racket high with face open and left hand still on the racket throat (although you cannot see it from this angle). Rosewall has shifted his grip about a quarter turn to the left; however, he does not put his thumb up the racket handle because this takes too much time in fast exchanges.

b

Frame b. The racket is being brought down to meet the ball with arm extending, weight shifting forward to the right foot, and left hand back for balance. Note how Rosewall has his eyes concentrated on the ball. He will stroke the ball slightly below waist height.

Frame c. Rosewall has just met the ball only slightly in front of his right foot in order to guide it down the line. The racket face is slightly open to give the ball underspin. His weight continues to shift forward, knees bent and racket arm extended to a comfortable distance with wrist firmly locked.

Frame d. Rosewall is finishing the stroke with his racket face open and his weight all on his right foot. The fact that his shoulders and hips have turned only a little and that the follow-through is straight ahead clearly indicates he has hit the ball down the line rather than cross court.

a

Figure 39

A Low Ralston Backhand

In this series of drawings we see Dennis Ralston getting down beautifully to a low, down-the-line backhand drive.

Frame a. The first position shown is at the moment that Ralston is stepping in to a low bouncing ball to his backhand. His left hand, having helped accomplish the full shoulder turn, is about to leave the racket, and his right arm is beginning to straighten. As in the case of Rosewall, his right shoulder is lowered to help meet the ball. This classic form is essentially the same for both players.

b

Frame b. Ralston is extending his arm with racket face open as he bends waist and knees to get down to the trajectory of the ball to better follow it into the center of his racket. The racket head has been lowered into position to meet the ball as it comes into view. The weight continues to shift forward.

c

Frame c. At the moment of impact Ralston gets his weight into the shot by turning his shoulders and transmitting his forward movement to his right foot. He strikes the ball a few inches in front of his right foot with the face of his racket open and his locked wrist leading the racket head a bit to lend sidespin as well as underspin in order to direct the ball down the line. Note that the eyes are fixed steadily on the ball.

d

Frame d. Here the stiff wrist is still just leading the open racket, with great arm extension, to show the basic characteristics of the down-the-line backhand. All his weight is now properly on his right foot.

Frame e. Ralston has completed the follow-through in approved manner with arm
extended and racket high above the shoulder. The fact that he hit the ball down the
line is shown clearly. First, as with Rosewall, his wrist has not rolled over and is
still leading the racket. Second, in following
the flight of the ball he is looking straight
down the line.

The backhand lob should be hit just as the forehand, except that it is almost always hit with underspin with an open racket face.

Both offensive and defensive lobs should be aimed as near the base line as possible. The defensive lob is usually hit higher than the offensive lob to give one a greater margin of error and to allow time to get back into position. Actually, the lob is an excellent shot which most young players would do well to utilize more often. An offensive lob to the backhand is difficult for any net player to handle. And even the high, deep, defensive lob is not easy to hit with an overhead, particularly if the wind and sun are playing tricks. Often the only safe play the net player has is to permit the ball to bounce and then hit a service stroke overhead.

Drop Shot

The drop shot is hit like a chop but with a short follow-through. The shot is a delicate one requiring great touch. The ball should clear the net with plenty to spare, yet bounce within about 8 feet of the net, and have so much backspin on it that it does not bound toward the retriever but falls dead. It takes plenty of practice to be able to employ this tricky shot with confidence.

Chop

The chop has gone out of style as a basic ground stroke, as it floats enough to give an advantage to an opponent at net. It is murder, however, against a base liner on a wet grass court with its skidding bounce. The chip, dink, and slice can be used from the base line, just as on return of service, to force the net player to volley up unless he or she is on top of the net, in which case you resort to the lob.

8

Summary

The game of singles in tennis is more than an athletic contest of strength, stamina, agility, and skill, it is also an intellectual contest. There is a defense for every attack and an attack for every defense, and often the more intelligent and adroit player can overcome the "stronger" player. This is because you develop tactical plans based on your own strengths and your opponent's weaknesses in order to force the opponent to accept battle under the least favorable conditions at every possible opportunity.

When one adds the intricacies of stroke production to the extensive tactical variations of tennis, there is little wonder that mastery of all of the secrets of the game becomes a very long and difficult task. But it is equally true that a real knowledge of a number of fundamentals of each will go a long way toward making a tennis player. Once these are clearly understood and kept continually in mind, the player can then concentrate on the finer points, such as depth and anticipation, which ultimately spell excellence. It is the purpose of this book to try to present the fundamentals in a manner to provide a useful and sound foundation for beginner and expert alike.

To begin this summary at the beginning, let us first review briefly the basic principles of stroke production.

Perhaps the single most important thing to remember is that all the great champions of past and present have had one thing in common: they made the game look ridiculously easy. While their style and grips and methods of meeting the ball varied in certain details, they all developed simple, fluid strokes which were a delight to behold. Every move was made with perfect footwork and balance and no stroke was cluttered with unnecessary motions.

This is the direction in which the aspiring player must move. To be sure, you can learn tennis up to a point by following the methods of the great. You can start by adopting the eastern grip and the basic backswing, follow-through, weight shift, and footwork of the champions until you can enjoy the game by keeping the ball in play with consistency. It is particularly important to get down to the ball (bend the knees) on ground strokes and volleys, keep your eye on the ball as you stroke it, and practice your toss to achieve a forcing serve. From this point on you have to develop your own style in detail, depending on the particular physical equipment you possess. Obviously, a small man cannot hit shots like the six footers. And even players having similar physiques can be recognized on a tennis court two blocks away by their differences in style. In developing your own game do not overlook the assistance of experienced coaches and professionals. It is usually far easier for such persons to spot flaws in your methods than for you to discover them yourself.

The serve is the single most important stroke in modern offensive tennis. A strong serve is a must—it puts the striker on the offensive, and should of itself open the door for wins in a staggering 40 percent of points by forcing weak returns of service or errors. The big serve is twice as effective on fast courts as on slow clay or composition courts.

The primary things to remember are to get the first serve in and to keep all serves deep. The experts accomplish both some 80 percent of the time. The real hallmark of a top server is a player who can keep the second serve deep. Good first serves and good deep deliveries, whether first or second serves, ultimately produce a won point in about 75 percent of the cases.

On fast courts the top players follow every serve rapidly to the net and attempt to volley any return away for a winner. First serves are usually aimed toward the side lines, to open up the court, and second serves at the backhand corner. On slow courts the server usually hits for the backhand corner and only occasionally follows serve in to the net position since returns of service are more effective on such surfaces.

To win in tennis you have to be able to break your opponent's service. In order to blunt his or her most important weapons, it is essential to develop a good return of service—one of the most difficult as well as important shots in the game. This you can do only if you pay attention to details. Receiving position is important—a foot or more inside the base line on a line bisecting the possible angle of service delivery is recommended. To be able to get your racket on the speeding ball, you must also work on anticipation of the type and direction of serve the opponent is about to hit. By far the most important thing, of course, is to get the ball back—if you don't, you have lost the point, and if you do, you have an almost even chance of ultimately winning. If you can control the ball, as well as get it back, you should try to hit it low against a net-rushing server to force a volley up, and deep to the base line against a server who stays back in order to keep him or her pinned back. The delight of all receivers is the "fat" serve that lands shallow in the service court. Such serves should be eaten alive by moving in and pounding them down the line or, occasionally, sharply cross court. Avoid returns to the center of the court, as they are easiest for the server to handle. Returns to the side lines should win 50 to 60 percent of the time, whereas returns to the middle will give the volleyer a 70 to 80 percent chance of winning. Whenever possible, the receiver should try to grab the offensive by taking the net. A determined receiver, equipped with nerve, audacity, good ground strokes, and the ability to mix up the direction, speed and spin of returns, can drive the server crazy by forcing him or her to work to the limit for every point.

Attack is the foundation of modern tennis. The percentages favor the attacker, and tennis is a percentage game. The net position is the best location from which to exploit the attack, as shown by the fact that net play accounts for close to one third of all points won. No longer can any player think of the volley and overhead as strokes reserved for the experts. Rather, these strokes represent the easiest possible way of finishing off a point once you have forced the opponent out of position. Volleying a return sharply gives the opponent no time to recover, whereas waiting on the base line for the ball affords plenty of time to amble back into position, as well as to glance around at all the beautiful girls in the gallery during the process. The clincher is that volleying is also superb fun.

The best volleyers prepare the path to the net properly by hitting a forcing approach shot to draw a weak, easy-to-volley return. Poor approach shots make the volleyer extremely vulnerable. The volley should really be thought of as a combination of a forcing approach shot followed by a volley. The most important things to remember are to keep the approach shots deep and, when you take the net, to move in close (within 6 to 9 feet) so you can volley down severely or angle the ball sharply. Always assume each volley will be returned and, as you anticipate the speed and direction, shift your volley position accordingly.

The toughest volley to make is the first volley, because it is stroked as you run in and must often be hit up from your shoe-tops, or hit when you are scrambling and reaching to the limit. Unless presented with an easy placement opportunity, the best tactic by far is to hit the first volley deep (within 8 to 10 feet of the base line). Few players can pass you from deep in the court, especially from the backhand side. In fact, the chances of winning the point after a deep first volley are about nine to one in your favor. If, on the other hand, you hit a shallow volley to the danger area in the middle of the court, disaster results—you will be passed or forced to err about six or seven out of ten times.

When both players are on the base line, there is one overriding rule—keep the ball deep. The whole base line game consists of fencing until you can force the opponent into hitting a ball short. This provides you with the opportunity of moving in and hitting a forcing shot, deep or angled, which you can turn into a winning point. (It is too risky to try to get in to the net from deep in the court.) Actually, about seven out of eight base line points are won after one of the players hits a short shot. The other player can then take advantage of this opening in two ways. In about two out of three cases the point is won with a forcing shot which will score a placement or elicit an error. In the third case the player can make a forcing shot, follow it in to the net, and then volley away the return for the point. During base line rallies, assume each shot will be returned and concentrate on anticipating its direction and depth so that you can move to the proper position.

Earlier we mentioned the need for the net player to volley the ball deep until there is an opening for a placement. If we consider this now from the standpoint of the defender, the importance of taking advantage of any short volleys will become evident. When the volley is within 10 feet of the base line, it is very difficult to pass the net player. About the best you can do is to try to force a volley up or, if he or she is on top of the net, a lob. Even so, you will win only about one out of four or five times. But if the volley lands between the service line and a point 10 feet from the base line, the tide should turn in your favor, provided you hit accurately while masking the direction of your shot. And if the volley lands within the service court, you should be able to pass the net player over 80 percent of the time on any ball you can reach. The short volley is obviously the true friend of the defender. Whenever you force the net player to hit a shallow volley, be prepared to take unerring advantage of the gift.

If required to pick the one most important factor in winning singles, we would unhesitatingly select that of keeping the ball in play. Errors are the killers in tennis. To emphasize this, let us look at the terrific erosion they produce:

Twenty-five percent of returns of service are errors. If the receiver can just return the serve, there is an almost even chance of winning the point.

Twenty-five percent of first volleys are errors. If the volleyer can just make the first volley, only 50 percent of the shots are returned.

If the receiver can just return service and return the first volley, there is a better than even chance of winning the point.

This explains why the steady player and the great getters are so hard to beat in singles.

To date all scoring information in tennis mentions only two types of errors—nets and outs. Actually, we think it is more proper to say there are three kinds of errors—nets, outs, and forced errors. In making this distinction we are following the system used in baseball, where a sufficiently difficult chance is not charged as an error against the fielder but is scored as a hit for the batter. When this is done in tennis, it provides a better picture of the actual play and the value of the forcing game. In normal scoring, you find that almost 60 percent of points are won on errors and 40 percent are earned through placements or service aces. The errors are almost equally divided between nets and outs. However, if you also consider forced errors in scoring you find the reverse is true—only 40 percent of points are won by errors, while an overwhelming 60 percent are won by earned points including forced errors. There is little doubt the forcing game is king.

Condition and fight are necessary ingredients for a well-rounded tennis game. Often they determine the outcome, especially in the final set of a long match. When you are tired you tend to lose concentration—improper selection of shots increases and errors start to pour off your racket. This is when courage is needed to fight your way back into the game. The determination not to lose is, more than any other single thing, what makes players like Evert and Connors great. And anyone who has ever watched Laver cannot help but notice how he cranks in that extra effort to lift his game whenever he gets behind.

There are tricks to both conditioning and fighting. Of course the international player must do roadwork, practice starting fast and running backward as well as forward (moving sideways and making quick changes of direction), eat properly, and get sufficient sleep. But even the weekend player can benefit from the less strenuous tricks of the trade—such things as wearing comfortable clothes, preventing tired feet through wearing a pair of cotton socks under his sweat socks, taking deep breaths when tired, and refraining from drinking much during the course of the match. We say this despite the fact that Dr. James Dwight, the father of American lawn tennis, recommended a spot of brandy in your water when tired! And when you are barely able to drag yourself around the court, there are ways of reviving yourself. One of the best ways we know of to renew the spirit is the method used by one of the greatest fighters in tennis history. When most downtrodden he revitalized himself by making an extra effort to put a decided spring in his walk and to concentrate on watching the ball. The combination of this spirited effort not only revived him but, at the same time, served to throw consternation into the mind and the game of his opponent. Small tricks of this type can be magical in their effect. When tired, remember to think!

Practice is essential to progress. Some top players began at a tender age by banging a ball against a backboard by the hour. At any tournament you will see young aspirants practicing ground strokes, volleys, and serves until dark, or as long as the officials will let them use the courts. A bit more practice, especially in the art of anticipation, would help most weekend players. The tournament players use practice to correct weaknesses in their games, not to try to win. And if you think you practice a lot, just remember that some champion players work out for as many as five sets on the morning of an important match!

Next to practice, the best way to sharpen your game is to play in tournaments. The experience of playing under pressure against various opponents adds the all-important ingredient of seasoning. Butterflies flutter in the stomachs of the best before a match. There is a bit of psychology even in walking on the court—Connors acts like a sure winner before he ever hits a ball. To be a good tournament player you have to develop the ability to avoid becoming upset by any distractions from the crowd or your opponent, or by decisions you think to be bad. If off form, often a grin at yourself will relax the tension.

The importance of true sportsmanship in bringing real enjoyment to the game of tennis can hardly be overemphasized. This entails not only devotion to such things as fair play and proper court manners, but also providing assistance to other players and to your local tennis association. Finally, it means going out of your way to thank those who also serve, but without glory—the umpire, linesmen, ball boys, and tournament officials.

In parting, we wish you the best of luck in your singles play—may all your tactics please the best of the critics and may all your bounces be true!